From our Holiday Kitchen

The ATCO Blue Flame Kitchen holiday cookbook is an annual tradition. We hope it will become well-used in your kitchen for all of your celebrations and entertaining year-round.

The staff at ATCO Blue Flame Kitchen, along with our management and fellow employees at ATCO Gas, would like to take this opportunity to wish you a happy and healthy holiday season.

The ATCO Blue Flame Kitchen trademark is your assurance that each recipe has been tested in our professional kitchens and meets the highest standards. As always, we have developed these recipes to reflect the latest culinary trends, and have worked to ensure that the ingredients for most are readily available in communities across Alberta.

There is more to our story than cookbooks and recipes. ATCO Blue Flame Kitchen has been providing household advice and tips on energy safety, conservation and efficiency for more than 80 years.

Now, there are more ways to connect with us than ever before. Visit us anytime online at www.atcoblueflamekitchen.com, or to speak directly with a professional home economist, call the ATCO Blue Flame Kitchen Answer Line toll-free Monday to Friday at 1.877.420.9090.

For information or to register for cooking classes and other programs available through the ATCO Blue Flame Kitchen Learning Centre in Calgary, call 403.245.7630. Class schedules are available on our website.

The staff of
ATCO Blue Flame Kitchen

10035 - 105 Street
Edmonton, Alberta T5J 2V6

909 - 11 Avenue SW
Calgary, Alberta T2R 1L8

Printed and bound in Calgary, Alberta, Canada

To contact the ATCO Blue Flame Kitchen Answer Line
from the Edmonton area, call 780.420.1010;
from Lloydminster, call toll-free 1.306.825.5010;
from other locations in Alberta, call toll-free 1.877.420.9090.

To contact the ATCO Blue Flame Kitchen Learning Centre
from the Calgary area, call 403.245.7630.

To purchase cookbooks, call the order desk toll-free 1.800.840.3393
or visit our website at www.atcoblueflamekitchen.com.

TABLE OF CONTENTS

RECIPE KEY

Tips for success with ATCO Blue Flame Kitchen recipes.

+ For best results, use good-quality ingredients.

+ Before starting to cook, read the recipe completely.

+ The ingredients are listed in the order in which they are used in the method.

+ Assemble the ingredients and prepare them as directed in the ingredient list before proceeding to the method.

+ Prepare pans and preheat oven before beginning to cook.

+ Measure liquids in glass or clear plastic liquid measuring cups.

+ Measure dry ingredients in nesting dry measuring cups (usually made of metal or plastic) that can be levelled off with a straightedge, such as a knife.

+ Measure flour by spooning, not scooping, it into a dry measuring cup. Level off with a straightedge without tapping or shaking cup.

+ Measure brown sugar by packing it firmly enough into a dry measuring cup so that it holds the shape of the cup when turned out.

+ Use golden brown sugar where specified and dark brown sugar where specified. If a recipe simply calls for packed brown sugar, use either type.

+ In recipes calling for butter, do not use soft tub margarine or vegetable oil as a substitute as this may adversely affect the final product.

+ Butter and cream cheese are allowed to soften at room temperature for easier creaming.

+ Egg whites will give a greater volume if allowed to stand at room temperature for 30 minutes before beating.

+ Whipping cream will whip faster if both bowl and beaters are chilled in the freezer for 15 minutes before whipping. Generally, cream is whipped to soft peaks when it is to be folded into a dessert base. When it is whipped enough to hold its shape, or stiff, it is perfect for use as a dessert garnish.

+ Use chocolate chips made from pure chocolate. All chocolate chips are formulated to keep their shape in baking and may not melt smoothly for use in cakes and tortes. Imitation chocolate-flavoured chips may be very difficult to melt.

+ Unless otherwise specified, do not use light (lite) products (cream cheese, sour cream, mayonnaise, peanut butter, etc.) as they may give poor results due to differences in fat and moisture content.

- Unless otherwise specified, assume that:
  - Flour is all-purpose; do not sift unless directed to in recipe. If other flour (unbleached, whole wheat, etc.) is substituted, there may be a change in texture.
  - Cake and pastry flour is sifted before measuring.
  - Sugar is granulated (white).
  - Icing sugar is not sifted before measuring.
  - Unsweetened cocoa powder is first measured and then sifted.
  - Honey is liquid, not creamed.
  - Molasses is fancy molasses.
  - Peanut butter is smooth.
  - Butter is salted.
  - Eggs are large.
  - Milk is 2% M.F. (milk fat); light cream is 10% M.F. (milk fat).
  - Low fat and regular sweetened condensed milk may be used interchangeably.
  - Yogurt is plain (unflavoured).
  - All fruits and vegetables are thoroughly washed before using.
  - Carrots, onions, parsnips, garlic and fresh ginger are peeled.
  - Salt is table salt; pepper is freshly ground black pepper.
  - Hot pepper sauce is Tabasco Pepper Sauce; Louisiana-style hot sauce is Frank's Red Hot Original Cayenne Pepper Sauce.
  - Firm and semi-soft cheeses, such as cheddar, mozzarella and Swiss, are freshly shredded.
  - Hard cheeses, such as Parmesan and Romano, are freshly grated.
  - Oil is canola; olive oil is extra virgin; sesame oil is light brown in colour.
  - Vanilla is pure vanilla extract.
- A baking pan refers to a metal pan, while a baking dish refers to a glass or ceramic dish.
- When measuring the dimensions of baking pans and baking dishes, measure the distance across the top from the inside rim on one side to the inside rim on the opposite side.
- Frypans may be classified in size as small, medium or large. Usually, small fypans are 5 – 8 inches (12.5 – 20 cm) in diameter; medium frypans are 9 – 10 inches (23 – 25 cm) in diameter; and large frypans are about 12 inches (30 cm) in diameter.
- Follow the doneness tests described in the recipes. Cooking times should be used only as a guideline.

The Cook's Glossary

Baste To spoon or brush melted fat, meat drippings or stock over food to keep it moist and add flavour during cooking.

Blanch To partially cook food using boiling water or steam, then immerse in ice water to stop the cooking process. Blanching is used to soften, to loosen skins (as in peaches and tomatoes) and to destroy enzymes and set colour of vegetables before freezing.

Braise To cook in a small amount of liquid in a tightly covered pan using low heat for a lengthy period of time to develop flavour and tenderize food.

Cream To beat an ingredient or combination of ingredients using a spoon, electric mixer or food processor until mixture is soft, smooth and creamy.

Cube To cut food into ½ – 1 inch (1.25 – 2.5 cm) cubes.

Deglaze To simmer a small amount of stock, wine or other liquid in the cooking pan after cooked food and excess fat is removed, thereby loosening browned bits left in bottom of pan. This incorporates solids and cooking juices into a gravy or sauce.

Dice To cut food into ⅛ – ¼ inch (3 – 6 mm) cubes.

Dredge To coat a food with a dry ingredient such as flour, crumbs, cornmeal or sugar.

Fold To gently combine ingredients without decreasing their volume. Folding is used to incorporate a light airy mixture such as whipped cream or beaten egg whites into a heavier mixture such as a custard.

Julienne To cut food into thin matchstick strips.

Mince To cut food into very small pieces.

Poach To cook food gently in barely simmering liquid over low heat.

Purée To grind, mash or liquefy food by using a blender, food processor, food mill or sieve until it is a fine pulp of soft, smooth consistency.

Reduce To boil a liquid (usually stock, wine or a sauce mixture) rapidly until the volume is reduced by evaporation, thereby thickening the consistency and intensifying the flavour.

Roux A mixture of fat and flour that is slowly cooked over low heat. It is used to thicken mixtures such as gravies, sauces and soups. The colour and flavour of the roux is determined by the length of the cooking time.

Sauté To cook food quickly in a small amount of fat in a frypan over direct heat.

Sear To brown meat quickly using high heat, either in a frypan, under a broiler, on a natural gas barbecue or in a very hot oven, to seal in juices of meat.

ALL ABOUT HAM

Selecting *Bone-in whole ham* is the cured and smoked whole leg of pork. This ham contains the whole muscle and may be cut and sold as smaller shank or butt portions. The rind may be partially or completely removed. Some of these hams are labelled fully cooked and are ready to serve, but they can also be heated and glazed. Others are labelled uncooked or partially cooked and must be cooked before eating. *Boneless hams* such as Old Fashioned, Black Forest, Honey and Toupie Style are processed ham products. They are usually ready to serve and easy to carve.

When purchasing a ham, make sure there is a good proportion of lean meat to fat. The outer fat covering should be firm and white.

+ *Bone-in hams* provide 2 – 3 servings per pound (500 g).

+ *Boneless hams* provide 3 – 4 servings per pound (500 g).

Storing Unless otherwise specified by a best-before date, refrigerate ham in its original wrapping for up to 7 days. If vacuum packaged, check package for best-before date. *Leftover cooked ham* should be refrigerated within 2 hours of cooking. Keep refrigerated for up to 4 days. For best quality, do not freeze ham either before or after cooking as freezing temperatures result in changes in flavour and texture. If necessary to freeze ham, wrap ham in moisture-proof wrapping and store in freezer for 1 – 2 months. Thaw in refrigerator before using. Plan to use thawed ham in cooked dishes such as casseroles and soups. Do not refreeze.

Cooking Follow recipe directions for baking a ham or use the following general method. If desired, remove rind from ham. Without cutting into the meat, score fat in a criss-cross fashion to make diamonds. Place ham, fat side up, on a rack in a roasting pan. Insert a meat thermometer into centre of thickest part of ham without touching bone.

+ For hams labelled fully cooked and ready to serve, bake, uncovered, at 325°F (160°C) for 12 – 15 minutes per pound (500 g) or until a meat thermometer registers 140°F (60°C).

+ For hams labelled uncooked or partially cooked, bake, uncovered, at 325°F (160°C) for 20 minutes per pound (500 g) or until a meat thermometer registers 160°F (71°C).

If ham is to be glazed, apply glaze during last 30 minutes of cooking. Transfer ham to a platter and cover with foil. Let stand for 10 – 15 minutes before carving.

TURKEY SAFETY

All equipment used for thawing, storing, preparing and serving turkey must be clean. Keep the following in mind when handling raw turkey:

* Wash hands thoroughly with hot soapy water for 20 seconds before, during and after handling and preparing raw turkey.

* Discard all wrappings that have been used to store raw turkey.

* Cutting boards used for preparing turkey must be in good condition. Cracks and crevices can harbour bacteria.

* Thoroughly wash all equipment, work surfaces and sink with hot soapy water after preparing raw turkey. Cutting boards should be scrubbed with a stiff brush. Follow by rinsing all equipment, work surfaces and sink with a solution of 1 tbsp (15 mL) chlorine bleach per quart (litre) of water. Air-dry to prevent recontamination of equipment, work surfaces and sink.

* Launder dishcloths and towels with hot water, detergent and chlorine bleach after handling raw turkey.

* Use a clean plate for serving cooked turkey.

Thawing Turkey To thaw turkey safely, use one of the following methods:

Refrigerator Method Leave turkey in original wrapping. Place on a tray; refrigerate. Allow a minimum of 5 hours/pound (10 hours/kg) for thawing.

Cold Water Method Leave turkey in original wrapping. Place in a large container filled with cold water. As turkey will float, cover top surface with a clean damp tea towel. Change water frequently to ensure it remains cold. Allow a minimum of 1 hour/pound (2 hours/kg) for thawing. Do not leave in cold water overnight. If necessary to continue thawing overnight, place turkey on a tray; refrigerate.

When turkey is thawed, remove giblets and neck from cavities; wash and store in a covered container in refrigerator. Wash turkey in cold salted water, pat dry and stuff cavity with paper towels. Place on a tray, cover with damp paper towels and plastic wrap; refrigerate until ready to cook. Cook turkey and giblets within 24 hours.

Storing Cooked Turkey and Gravy Remove turkey meat from carcass as soon as possible. Refrigerate meat for up to 3 days or freeze for up to 3 months. If making soup, use carcass within 24 hours or freeze for up to 1 month. Leftover gravy may be refrigerated for up to 2 days or frozen for up to 1 month.

ROASTING TURKEY

*Follow recipe directions for roasting a turkey or use the following general method. Roast turkey at 425°F (220°C) for the first 30 minutes, then reduce temperature to 325°F (160°C) for remainder of the cooking time. Cooking times below are approximate and are for **unstuffed** thawed or fresh whole turkeys and turkey halves. **Do not interrupt roasting time or partially cook at one time to complete later.***

Whole Turkey (Thawed)	Total Cooking Time
10 lb (4.5 kg)	$2^3/_4 - 3$ hours
15 lb (7.0 kg)	$3 - 3^1/_2$ hours
20 lb (9.0 kg)	$4 - 4^1/_2$ hours
26 lb (12.0 kg)	$4^1/_2 - 5$ hours

Whole Turkey (Fresh)	Add 3 minutes/lb (5 minutes/kg) to above times.

Turkey Halves	
4 lb (1.8 kg)	$2 - 2^1/_2$ hours
8 lb (3.5 kg)	$3^1/_2 - 4$ hours
12 lb (5.5 kg)	$4 - 4^1/_2$ hours

◆   ◆   ◆

Roast turkey breast at 325°F (160°C) for entire cooking time.

Turkey Breast	
5 lb (2.3 kg) bone-in	$2^1/_2 - 3$ hours
5 lb (2.3 kg) boneless	$3 - 3^1/_2$ hours

Test for Doneness Using a meat thermometer is the most accurate method to judge when turkey is done. Insert meat thermometer into the middle of thick thigh muscle parallel to bone and next to body or into thickest muscle of breast. Be sure thermometer does not touch bone. When turkey is cooked, the final reading should be 180 – 185°F (82 – 85°C) in the thigh and 170 – 175°F (77 – 80°C) in the breast. If a meat thermometer is not available, pinch thick muscle of drumstick or breast between cloth- or paper towel-protected fingers; meat should feel soft. Leg will move easily when twisted. Another check is to run a long-tined fork into thick muscle; meat should feel tender and juice should show no pink tinge.

NOTES

BREAKFAST AND BRUNCH

Quiche Lorraine (page 12)

QUICHE LORRAINE

This classic quiche can be prepared using our Foolproof Pastry (recipe on page 109).

6 slices bacon, chopped
2 cups (500 mL) thinly sliced onions
Pastry for a 9 inch (23 cm) single-crust pie
Flour (for dusting surface)
4 eggs
¼ tsp (1 mL) salt
⅛ tsp (0.5 mL) freshly ground pepper
Pinch nutmeg
½ cup (125 mL) milk
½ cup (125 mL) whipping cream
2 cups (500 mL) shredded Swiss cheese

Cook bacon in a medium frypan over medium heat until browned and crisp. Remove from heat.

Remove bacon with a slotted spoon; drain bacon on paper towels. Drain off all but 1 tbsp (15 mL) fat from frypan. Return frypan to medium heat. Add onions and sauté until softened, about 5 minutes. Remove from heat; set aside.

Preheat oven to 375°F (190°C). To prepare crust, roll out pastry on a lightly floured surface; fit into a 9 inch (23 cm) pie plate, allowing for ½ inch (1.25 cm) overhang. Trim, fold and flute edges of pastry. Prick bottom of crust all over with a fork. Line bottom of crust with a piece of parchment paper and fill crust with pie weights, dried beans or raw rice. This helps prevent the crust from shrinking or puffing up during baking.

Bake for 10 minutes. Remove pie plate from oven. Remove pie weights and parchment paper. Prick bottom of crust all over with a fork.

Continue baking for 10 minutes or until crust is light golden around edges. Meanwhile, whisk together eggs, salt, pepper and nutmeg in a bowl. Whisk in milk and cream until blended; set aside. Remove pie plate from oven.

Sprinkle bottom of crust with bacon. Top with onions. Sprinkle with cheese. Pour egg mixture evenly over top.

Continue baking for 35 minutes or until a knife inserted in centre comes out clean. Let stand for 10 minutes before serving. *Serves 6 – 8.*

GRAPEFRUIT WITH RUM RAISIN SYRUP

¼ cup (50 mL) sugar
¼ cup (50 mL) water
⅓ cup (75 mL) dark rum
⅓ cup (75 mL) raisins
4 large red grapefruit, peeled and sectioned
2 tbsp (25 mL) sliced almonds, toasted

To prepare syrup, combine sugar and water in a small saucepan. Bring to a boil over medium heat, stirring until sugar is dissolved. Boil for 1 minute. Remove from heat.

Combine rum and raisins in a small bowl. Stir in syrup. Cover and let stand at room temperature for 8 hours.

Place grapefruit sections in a bowl. Pour rum mixture over grapefruit and toss gently to combine. Sprinkle with almonds. *Serves 6 – 8.*

SAFETY MATTERS

ATCO Gas provides information and safety checks to assist customers in using natural gas safely and wisely.

Call our Customer Assistance Centre at 310.5678 or visit www.atcogas.com for information.

SOUTHWESTERN BREAKFAST WRAPS

4 eggs
½ tsp (2 mL) hot pepper sauce
¼ tsp (1 mL) salt
⅛ tsp (0.5 mL) freshly ground pepper
2 tbsp (25 mL) milk
4 whole wheat flour tortillas (9 inch/23 cm)
1 tbsp (15 mL) butter
½ cup (125 mL) canned black beans, rinsed and drained
1 cup (250 mL) shredded Monterey Jack cheese
¼ cup (50 mL) thinly sliced green onion
¼ cup (50 mL) salsa
¼ cup (50 mL) sour cream, optional

Preheat oven to 350°F (180°C). Whisk together eggs, hot pepper sauce, salt and pepper. Whisk in milk until blended; set aside. Wrap tortillas in foil.

Bake wrapped tortillas for 10 minutes. Meanwhile, melt butter in a large nonstick frypan over medium heat. Add egg mixture and cook, uncovered, lifting edges of eggs occasionally with a spatula, allowing uncooked egg to run underneath, until eggs are almost cooked. Stir in beans and continue cooking, uncovered, until eggs are cooked through. Do not overcook. Remove from heat and stir in cheese.

Remove wrapped tortillas from oven; unwrap tortillas. Spoon egg mixture on centre of tortillas, dividing equally. Top each with green onion, salsa and sour cream, dividing equally. Roll up tortillas to enclose filling. Serve immediately. *Serves 4.*

Southwestern Breakfast Wraps

SEPARATING AN EGG

To separate an egg, crack it against a hard surface and break the shell into two equal pieces. Working over a bowl, allow the egg white to fall into the bowl while carefully passing the egg yolk back and forth from one half of the shell to the other. It is important to keep the yolk intact as any yolk falling into the white will interfere with the white's ability to whip successfully. Transfer the yolk to a separate bowl.

VEGETARIAN ROULADE

1 tbsp (15 mL) butter
1½ cups (375 mL) sliced mushrooms
½ cup (125 mL) chopped onion
½ cup (125 mL) diced green bell pepper
½ cup (125 mL) diced red bell pepper
1 tbsp (15 mL) chopped fresh parsley
¼ tsp (1 mL) oregano, crumbled
½ tsp (2 mL) salt, divided
½ tsp (2 mL) freshly ground pepper, divided
Flour (for dusting baking sheet)
6 eggs, separated
3 tbsp (40 mL) flour
½ cup (125 mL) shredded cheddar cheese, divided

To prepare filling, melt butter in a medium frypan over medium heat. Add mushrooms, onion and bell peppers; sauté until softened, about 5 minutes. Stir in parsley, oregano, ¼ tsp (1 mL) salt and ¼ tsp (1 mL) pepper. Remove from heat; cool.

Preheat oven to 350°F (180°C). Line a 10x15 inch (25x38 cm) rimmed baking sheet with wax paper; grease wax paper and dust with flour.

To make soufflé, use medium speed of an electric mixer and beat egg whites until stiff but not dry. In a bowl, beat together egg yolks, 3 tbsp (40 mL) flour, remaining ¼ tsp (1 mL) salt and remaining ¼ tsp (1 mL) pepper. Fold a quarter of beaten egg whites into yolk mixture to lighten. Gently fold in remaining beaten egg whites. Spread mixture evenly in prepared pan.

Bake until top springs back when lightly touched, about 8 – 10 minutes. Run a spatula around sides of pan to loosen. Turn soufflé out onto a clean tea towel. Carefully remove wax paper. Trim edges of soufflé if necessary. Starting with a long edge, roll soufflé and towel together jelly-roll fashion. Cool on a rack for 30 minutes.

Unroll soufflé and spread with filling, leaving a ½ inch (1.25 cm) border around edges. Sprinkle with half of cheese. Roll up soufflé to enclose filling. Place soufflé, seam side down, on a lightly greased rimmed baking sheet. May be prepared to this point and refrigerated for up to 24 hours.

Remove baking sheet from refrigerator and let stand for 30 minutes. Meanwhile, preheat oven to 375°F (190°C). Sprinkle top of soufflé with remaining cheese.

Bake for 12 – 15 minutes or until light golden. Slice and serve. *Serves 6 – 8.*

FRUIT SALAD WITH BANANA SMOOTHIE DRESSING

¾ cup (175 mL) chopped banana
¾ cup (175 mL) plain yogurt
2 tbsp (25 mL) thawed frozen orange juice concentrate
1 tbsp (15 mL) honey
1 tsp (5 mL) vanilla
8 cups (2 L) assorted fresh fruit

To prepare dressing, place banana, yogurt, orange juice concentrate, honey and vanilla in a blender; purée until smooth. May be refrigerated for up to 24 hours. Stir before using.

Combine fruit in a large bowl. Pour dressing over fruit and toss to combine. Serve immediately. *Serves 6 – 8.*

 Cook's Note: *ATCO Blue Flame Kitchen used cubed grapefruit segments, cubed orange segments, cubed peeled apples, cubed peeled kiwi fruit, blueberries and seedless red grapes for the fresh fruit in this recipe.*

DID YOU KNOW?

After using part of a can of frozen juice concentrate in a recipe, you can reconstitute the remainder to use as a beverage. In general, combine 1 part juice concentrate with 3 parts water.

PEPPERY GLAZED BACON

1 lb (500 g) thick-sliced bacon
½ – 1 tsp (2 – 5 mL) freshly ground pepper
¼ cup (50 mL) Thai sweet chili sauce

Preheat oven to 375°F (190°C). Line a large rimmed baking sheet with foil or parchment paper. Place a rack on top.

Place bacon on rack in prepared pan. Sprinkle top of bacon slices with pepper.

Bake for 20 minutes. Remove pan from oven and brush top of bacon slices with chili sauce.

Reduce oven temperature to 350°F (180°C). Continue baking until bacon is glazed and crisp, about 15 minutes. Serve immediately. *Serves 6 – 8.*

ROSEMARY BREAKFAST POTATOES WITH YAMS

4 cups (1 L) cubed peeled yellow potatoes (1 inch/2.5 cm)
4 cups (1 L) cubed peeled yams (1 inch/2.5 cm)
¼ cup (50 mL) butter, melted
1 tbsp (15 mL) chopped fresh rosemary
1 tsp (5 mL) salt
½ tsp (2 mL) onion powder
½ tsp (2 mL) freshly ground pepper

Preheat oven to 375°F (190°C). Line a large rimmed baking sheet with nonstick foil.

Combine all ingredients in a large bowl; toss until potatoes and yams are coated. Place potato mixture in a single layer in prepared pan.

Bake, uncovered, turning once, for 1 hour or until potatoes and yams are tender and lightly browned. *Serves 8.*

Peppery Glazed Bacon, Rosemary Breakfast Potatoes with Yams

Storing brown sugar in an airtight container will help prevent the brown sugar from drying out and hardening. If your brown sugar has hardened, place it in an airtight container or a zip-lock plastic bag and place a few slices of apple or a slice of fresh bread on top. After a few days the brown sugar should soften. Remove and discard the apple or bread as they can spoil.

OVERNIGHT CARAMEL FRENCH TOAST

1½ cups (375 mL) packed brown sugar
¾ cup (175 mL) butter
⅓ cup (75 mL) white corn syrup
8 – 10 slices French bread, 1½ inches (3.75 cm) thick
4 eggs
2½ cups (625 mL) homogenized milk
1 tbsp (15 mL) vanilla
¼ tsp (1 mL) salt
⅛ tsp (0.5 mL) nutmeg
2 tbsp (25 mL) sugar
1 tsp (5 mL) cinnamon

Combine brown sugar, butter and corn syrup in a medium heavy saucepan. Cook over medium heat, stirring constantly, for 5 minutes or until mixture is bubbly. Pour mixture evenly over bottom of a greased 9x13x2 inch (23x33x5 cm) baking dish. Arrange bread slices on top of brown sugar mixture. Bread slices should fit tightly.

Whisk together eggs, milk, vanilla, salt and nutmeg. Pour egg mixture evenly over bread slices. Cover and refrigerate overnight.

Remove baking dish from refrigerator and let stand for 20 – 30 minutes. Meanwhile, preheat oven to 350°F (180°C). Combine sugar and cinnamon; sprinkle over bread slices.

Bake, uncovered, for 45 – 50 minutes or until puffed and a knife inserted in centre comes out clean. Serve immediately. *Serves 8 – 10.*

CRISPY RAISED WAFFLES

These waffles are raised with yeast. They cook up crispy on the outside and light and tender on the inside.

½ cup (125 mL) warm water (100 – 110°F/38 – 43°C)
2 tsp (10 mL) active dry yeast
1 tsp (5 mL) sugar
2 cups (500 mL) flour
1 tsp (5 mL) salt
⅛ tsp (0.5 mL) baking soda
2 cups (500 mL) warm milk (100 – 110°F/38 – 43°C)
½ cup (125 mL) butter, melted and cooled
2 eggs
Maple or pancake syrup

Combine warm water, yeast and sugar in a large bowl. Let stand until foamy, about 5 minutes. Meanwhile, combine flour, salt and baking soda. Whisk warm milk, cooled melted butter and eggs into yeast mixture. Whisk in flour mixture until blended. Mixture will be thin. Cover with oiled wax paper and a clean damp tea towel. Let rise in a warm draft-free place until doubled in volume, about 45 minutes.

Cook in a preheated greased waffle iron according to manufacturer's instructions until golden brown. Serve with syrup. *Makes 10 – 12.*

www.atcoblueflamekitchen.com

Visit the ATCO Blue Flame Kitchen website to sign up for our monthly newsletter and access a large selection of recipes. Also, check out our website for seasonal information on everything from holiday entertaining to turkey and the trimmings.

SAFETY MATTERS

When cooking on a natural gas range, look for the blue flame. While flecks of orange are okay, if your flame is yellow and flickering, have it checked by a qualified technician.

For more safety tips, visit www.atcogas.com.

CINNAMON-SCENTED BUTTERMILK SYRUP

¾ cup (175 mL) buttermilk
¾ cup (175 mL) sugar
½ cup (125 mL) packed golden brown sugar
½ cup (125 mL) butter
2 tbsp (25 mL) honey
1 tsp (5 mL) baking soda
⅛ tsp (0.5 mL) cinnamon

Place all ingredients in a large nonreactive saucepan. Bring to a boil over medium heat, stirring frequently. Mixture will foam. Reduce heat and boil gently, stirring frequently, until slightly thickened, about 7 minutes. Serve warm with pancakes, waffles or French toast. May be refrigerated for up to 3 days. *Makes about 1½ cups (375 mL).*

PUMPKIN CREAM CHEESE SPREAD

8 oz (250 g) cream cheese, softened
½ cup (125 mL) canned pure pumpkin
⅓ cup (75 mL) icing sugar
1 tsp (5 mL) vanilla
½ tsp (2 mL) cinnamon
⅛ tsp (0.5 mL) ground ginger
⅛ tsp (0.5 mL) nutmeg
Dash ground cloves

Using medium speed of an electric mixer, beat together cream cheese and pumpkin until smooth. Beat in remaining ingredients (icing sugar through cloves) until blended. Cover and refrigerate for up to 2 days. Use as a spread for toasted bagels or muffins. *Makes 1½ cups (375 mL).*

STARTERS

Blueberry Baked Brie (page 24)

BLUEBERRY BAKED BRIE

1 tbsp (15 mL) oil
¼ cup (50 mL) finely chopped onion
1 tsp (5 mL) grated fresh ginger
1 clove garlic, finely chopped
1 cup (250 mL) fresh or frozen blueberries
¼ cup (50 mL) chopped peeled Granny Smith apple
3 tbsp (40 mL) dried blueberries
3 tbsp (40 mL) water
1 tbsp (15 mL) white wine vinegar
1 tbsp (15 mL) sugar
1 tsp (5 mL) grated lemon peel
¼ tsp (1 mL) cinnamon
¼ tsp (1 mL) freshly ground pepper
1 tbsp (15 mL) fresh lemon juice
1 round (450 g) brie cheese
3 tbsp (40 mL) sliced almonds, toasted

To prepare chutney, heat oil in a small nonreactive saucepan over medium heat. Add onion and sauté until softened, about 5 minutes. Add ginger and garlic; sauté for 30 seconds. Add next 9 ingredients (blueberries through pepper). Bring to a boil. Reduce heat and simmer, covered, stirring occasionally, for 15 minutes. Meanwhile, preheat oven to 325°F (160°C).

Uncover chutney and simmer, stirring occasionally, until thickened, about 8 – 9 minutes. Remove from heat and stir in lemon juice.

Score top of brie in a criss-cross fashion to make diamonds. Place brie in a baking dish that fits it almost exactly. Spoon chutney over brie.

Bake, covered, for 20 – 25 minutes or until brie is bubbly and heated through. Top with almonds. Serve with baguette slices or crackers. *Serves 8.*

SPIKED DRUMS

4 tsp (20 mL) ground cumin
1 tsp (5 mL) lemon pepper
1 tsp (5 mL) paprika
½ tsp (2 mL) cayenne pepper
½ tsp (2 mL) garlic powder
¼ tsp (1 mL) salt
3 lb (1.5 kg) chicken wing drumettes

Preheat oven to 400°F (200°C). Line a large rimmed baking sheet with nonstick foil. Place a rack on top.

Combine all ingredients except chicken in a small bowl. Place half of seasoning mixture in a heavy zip-lock plastic bag. Add half of chicken to seasoning mixture in bag. Seal bag and shake to coat. Place chicken in a single layer on rack in prepared pan. Repeat procedure with remaining seasoning mixture and chicken.

Bake, uncovered, turning once, for 50 – 55 minutes or until golden brown. *Makes about 36.*

ENERGY MATTERS

Plan to use the self-cleaning feature of your gas oven right after regular cooking. Less energy will be required to reach cleaning temperature because the oven is already hot.

For more energy saving ideas, visit www.atcoenergysense.com.

FREEZER ANTIPASTO

This antipasto cannot be safely home canned because of its low-acid ingredients.

1 cup (250 mL) olive oil
1 cup (250 mL) chopped onion
4 cups (1 L) small cauliflower florets
1½ cups (375 mL) diced green bell peppers
1 cup (250 mL) diced celery
1 can (10 oz/284 mL) sliced mushrooms, drained
3½ cups (875 mL) ketchup
1 bottle (455 mL) tomato-based chili sauce
½ cup (125 mL) white wine vinegar
⅓ cup (75 mL) chopped fresh parsley
2 tbsp (25 mL) fresh lemon juice
1 tsp (5 mL) basil, crumbled
1 tsp (5 mL) oregano, crumbled
1 tsp (5 mL) freshly ground pepper
¼ tsp (1 mL) ground cloves
⅛ tsp (0.5 mL) cayenne pepper
3 bay leaves
2 cloves garlic, finely chopped
1 jar (14 oz/398 mL) sliced pitted ripe olives, drained
1 jar (375 mL) pimiento-stuffed olives, drained and halved crosswise
1 jar (375 mL) sweet pickled onions, drained and halved crosswise
2 cans (170 g each) solid white tuna, drained and broken into chunks
1 can (106 g) broken shrimp, drained
2 cans (50 g each) anchovies, drained and chopped
1 jar (2 oz/57 mL) sliced pimientos, drained and chopped
¼ cup (50 mL) drained capers

Heat oil in a Dutch oven over medium heat. Add onion and sauté for
2 minutes. Add cauliflower, green peppers, celery and mushrooms; sauté
for 5 minutes. Stir in next 12 ingredients (ketchup through garlic). Bring

to a boil. Reduce heat and simmer, uncovered, stirring occasionally, for 10 minutes. Remove and discard bay leaves.

Stir in remaining ingredients (ripe olives through capers) and return to a boil. Reduce heat and simmer, uncovered, stirring occasionally, until mixture is slightly thickened, about 5 minutes. Remove from heat and cool quickly. To cool quickly, place pan in a sink of ice water and stir antipasto frequently to allow steam to escape. Do not allow ice water to enter pan.

Spoon cooled antipasto into freezer containers and freeze for up to 3 months. Thaw antipasto in refrigerator. Thawed antipasto may be refrigerated for up to 3 days. *Makes 16 cups (4 L).*

TURKISH RED PEPPER DIP

½ cup (125 mL) chopped drained canned roasted red peppers,
   patted dry
¼ cup (50 mL) chopped toasted walnuts
½ cup (125 mL) soft fresh bread crumbs
1 tbsp (15 mL) fresh lemon juice
1 tbsp (15 mL) olive oil
½ – 1 tsp (2 – 5 mL) ground cumin
¼ tsp (1 mL) red pepper flakes
1 clove garlic, crushed

Place roasted peppers and walnuts in a food processor; process, using an on/off motion, until coarsely chopped. Add remaining ingredients (bread crumbs through garlic); process, using an on/off motion, until almost smooth. Cover and refrigerate for at least 2 hours or up to 24 hours. Stir before serving. Serve with pita chips. *Makes ¾ cup (175 mL).*

SAFETY MATTERS

Make sure your chimney and flue vents are free from blockages. This will prevent the buildup of carbon monoxide in your home.

For more safety tips, visit www.atcogas.com.

ROSEMARY BISCOTTI

This cocktail biscotti is delicious to serve as an hors d'oeuvre along with a glass of wine.

    1¾ cups (425 mL) flour
    2 tsp (10 mL) baking powder
    ½ tsp (2 mL) freshly ground pepper
    ¼ cup (50 mL) butter, softened
    2 tbsp (25 mL) olive oil
    ⅓ cup (75 mL) sugar
    1 tbsp (15 mL) chopped fresh rosemary or 1 tsp (5 mL) dried rosemary, crumbled
    2 eggs
    ½ cup (125 mL) chopped walnuts or pecans

Preheat oven to 375°F (190°C). Combine flour, baking powder and pepper in a bowl; set aside.

Using medium speed of an electric mixer, beat together butter and oil until fluffy. Add sugar and rosemary; beat until combined. Beat in eggs until blended. Stir in flour mixture. Fold in walnuts.

Divide dough in half. On a lightly floured surface, shape each half into a 9x2 inch (23x5 cm) log. Place logs on a greased cookie sheet and flatten slightly.

Bake for 25 – 30 minutes or until light golden. Cool logs on cookie sheet on a rack for 1 hour.

Preheat oven to 325°F (160°C). Transfer logs to a cutting board. Using a sharp knife, cut each log diagonally into 12 – 15 slices. Place slices, cut side down, on cookie sheets.

Bake for 10 minutes. Remove cookie sheets from oven. Turn slices over and continue baking for 8 – 10 minutes or until crisp. Remove from cookie sheets and cool biscotti on racks. Store in an airtight container in a cool dry place for up to 1 week. May be frozen. *Makes 2 – 2½ dozen.*

Rosemary Biscotti, Turkish Red Pepper Dip (page 27)

*Try these simple decorating tips
at your next holiday dinner party.
Place a tree ornament at each place
setting as a small gift for each guest.
Use festive ribbon to tie a bow
around napkins and the stem of
wine glasses.*

BEEF WELLINGTON TARTS

2 tbsp (25 mL) butter
2 cups (500 mL) finely chopped mushrooms
½ cup (125 mL) finely chopped onion
½ tsp (2 mL) salt
¼ tsp (1 mL) freshly ground pepper
2 tbsp (25 mL) brandy
¼ tsp (1 mL) nutmeg
¾ lb (0.375 kg) beef tenderloin
1 pkg (397 g) frozen puff pastry, thawed
Flour (for dusting surface)
¼ cup (50 mL) liver sausage
Béarnaise Sauce (recipe on page 31)

Melt butter in a medium frypan over medium heat. Add mushrooms, onion, salt and pepper; cook, stirring frequently, until mushrooms are browned and liquid is evaporated, about 7 minutes. Stir in brandy and nutmeg; cook, stirring, until liquid is evaporated. Remove from heat; set aside.

Preheat oven to 400°F (200°C). Cut beef into 24 cubes, each about ¾ inch (2 cm); set aside.

Divide pastry in half. On a lightly floured surface, roll out each half into a 10 inch (25 cm) square. Using a floured 2½ inch (6.25 cm) round cookie cutter, cut each half into 12 rounds. Press each round into a mini muffin cup. For each pastry shell, spoon about ½ tsp (2 mL) of mushroom mixture onto bottom. Top with about ½ tsp (2 mL) liver sausage and place 1 cube of beef on top.

Bake for 15 minutes or until pastry is golden brown, beef is cooked and juices are bubbly. Top each with about 1 tsp (5 mL) Béarnaise Sauce. Serve immediately. *Makes 24.*

 Cook's Note: *ATCO Blue Flame Kitchen used part of a 125 g package of Grimm's Fine Liver Sausage in this recipe.*

BÉARNAISE SAUCE

2 egg yolks
1 tbsp (15 mL) white wine vinegar
1 tbsp (15 mL) water
½ tsp (2 mL) tarragon, crumbled
⅛ tsp (0.5 mL) white pepper
⅓ cup (75 mL) butter, melted

Using medium speed of an electric mixer, beat egg yolks in a medium stainless steel bowl until pale yellow in colour, about 1 minute. Beat in vinegar, water, tarragon and white pepper until mixture is frothy, about 30 seconds.

Set bowl over a saucepan of simmering water. Do not allow water to touch bowl. Using low speed of an electric mixer, beat until mixture is thickened, frothy and pale in colour, about 1½ minutes. Remove bowl from saucepan.

Gradually beat in melted butter, beating until blended. Serve immediately. Do not keep leftover sauce. *Makes ⅔ cup (150 mL).*

GOAT CHEESE AND PISTACHIO SPREAD

2 logs (150 g each) soft goat cheese
½ cup (125 mL) butter, softened
2 tbsp (25 mL) finely chopped green onion
1 clove garlic, finely chopped
¼ cup (50 mL) chopped shelled roasted pistachios
Freshly ground pepper

Beat together cheese, butter, green onion and garlic until blended. Stir in pistachios. Season to taste with pepper. Cover and refrigerate for up to 2 days. Do not freeze. Serve with baguette slices. *Makes 2 cups (500 mL).*

DID YOU KNOW?

About ½ cup (125 mL) pistachios in their shells yields ¼ cup (50 mL) shelled pistachios.

PITTING AN AVOCADO

To pit an avocado, first cut the avocado lengthwise in half around the pit. Twist the halves in opposite directions to separate. The pit will stay in one of the halves. Cut each in half again to make quarters; separate. The pit can then be easily removed from its section.

BAJA SHRIMP COCKTAIL

½ cup (125 mL) diced seeded Roma tomatoes
¼ cup (50 mL) thinly sliced green onion
¼ cup (50 mL) chopped fresh cilantro
¼ cup (50 mL) tomato-based chili sauce
¼ cup (50 mL) fresh lime juice
1 tsp (5 mL) hot pepper sauce
1 lb (500 g) cooked small shrimp, rinsed and patted dry
2 ripe avocados, halved, pitted, peeled and cubed
4 cups (1 L) shredded iceberg lettuce

Combine first 6 ingredients (tomatoes through hot pepper sauce). Stir in shrimp and avocados. May be prepared to this point and refrigerated for up to 2 hours.

For each serving, place ½ cup (125 mL) shredded lettuce in a sherbet glass or on a small plate. Top each serving with shrimp mixture. *Serves 8.*

BAKED CRAB DIP IN A BREAD SHELL

1 round loaf bread (8 inch/20 cm)
2 cups (500 mL) mayonnaise
2 cups (500 mL) shredded Monterey Jack cheese
1 cup (250 mL) thinly sliced green onions
½ cup (125 mL) drained capers
1 can (120 g) crabmeat, drained, rinsed and flaked
⅛ tsp (0.5 mL) cayenne pepper
French bread cubes (1½ inch/3.75 cm)

Preheat oven to 350°F (180°C). Slice 1 inch (2.5 cm) off top of bread; set top aside. Hollow out bread, leaving a 1 inch (2.5 cm) thick shell; set shell aside. Tear or cut bread insides into bite-size pieces; reserve for dipping.

Combine next 6 ingredients (mayonnaise through cayenne pepper). Spoon mayonnaise mixture into bread shell. Replace top of bread. Wrap bread in foil.

Bake for 1 – 1¼ hours or until heated through. Unwrap bread and place on a serving dish. Serve with reserved bread pieces and French bread cubes. *Serves 8 – 10.*

 Cook's Note: *Check crabmeat carefully for any small pieces of shell and cartilage; remove and discard.*

BACON AND CHEESE STUFFED TOMATOES

50 – 60 cherry tomatoes
½ cup (125 mL) mayonnaise
⅓ cup (75 mL) crumbled cooked bacon
⅓ cup (75 mL) finely chopped green onions
¼ cup (50 mL) freshly grated Parmesan cheese
2 tbsp (25 mL) finely chopped celery
2 tbsp (25 mL) finely chopped fresh parsley
⅛ tsp (0.5 mL) freshly ground pepper

Cut a thin slice off top of each tomato; discard slices. Using a small melon baller or small spoon, scoop pulp out of tomatoes, leaving a ⅛ inch (3 mm) thick shell; discard pulp. Invert tomato shells onto several layers of paper towels. Let stand for 20 – 30 minutes. Meanwhile, to prepare filling, combine remaining ingredients (mayonnaise through pepper). Spoon filling into a pastry bag fitted with a large tip.

Pipe filling into tomato shells. Alternatively, filling may be spooned into tomato shells. Cover and refrigerate for up to 4 hours. *Makes 50 – 60.*

PARMESAN CHEESE RIND

After grating Parmesan cheese, there will be rind left with some of the cheese still attached. Rather than throwing it out, the rind may be added at the beginning of cooking a spaghetti sauce or soup. The rind will add to the flavour of the finished dish. Remember to remove the rind before serving.

WILD MUSHROOM TART

1 cup (250 mL) boiling water
1 pkg (14 g) dried porcini mushrooms
¼ cup (50 mL) butter
3 cups (750 mL) sliced cremini mushrooms (brown mushrooms)
¼ cup (50 mL) finely chopped onion
2 tbsp (25 mL) brandy
Butter Pastry (recipe on page 35)
Flour (for dusting surface)
⅔ cup (150 mL) shredded Swiss cheese, divided
1 egg
2 egg yolks
2 tbsp (25 mL) chopped fresh parsley
½ tsp (2 mL) thyme, crumbled
¼ tsp (1 mL) salt
¼ tsp (1 mL) freshly ground pepper
⅛ tsp (0.5 mL) nutmeg
¾ cup (175 mL) whipping cream

Pour boiling water over porcini mushrooms. Let stand for 30 minutes.

Drain porcini mushrooms through a sieve into a bowl, pressing to extract as much liquid as possible; reserve liquid. Rinse porcini mushrooms; pat dry with paper towels. Chop porcini mushrooms; set aside. Strain reserved liquid through a coffee filter-lined sieve into a bowl; set aside.

Melt butter in a large frypan over medium heat. Add porcini and cremini mushrooms; sauté until golden brown, about 10 minutes. Add onion and sauté for 2 minutes. Add strained liquid and brandy. Bring to a boil. Boil until liquid is almost evaporated, about 5 minutes. Remove from heat and cool.

To prepare crust, roll out chilled Butter Pastry on a lightly floured surface into a 12 inch (30 cm) round. Carefully transfer pastry to a 9 inch (23 cm) tart pan with a removable bottom. Trim edges, leaving a 1 inch (2.5 cm) overhang. Fold overhang in, pressing gently to form sides of crust. Press edges of pastry to raise crust ⅛ inch (3 mm) above pan. Refrigerate for 30 minutes.

Preheat oven to 375°F (190°C). Remove pan from refrigerator. Prick bottom of crust all over with a fork. Line crust with parchment paper, leaving a 1 inch (2.5 cm) overhang. Fill crust with pie weights, dried beans or raw rice. This helps prevent the crust from shrinking or puffing up during baking. Place pan on a rimmed baking sheet.

Bake until crust is light golden around edges, about 15 minutes. Remove baking sheet with pan from oven. Remove pie weights and parchment paper. Sprinkle half of cheese over crust. Spread mushroom mixture evenly over cheese. Whisk together next 7 ingredients (egg through nutmeg). Whisk in cream. Pour egg mixture evenly over top of mushroom mixture. Sprinkle with remaining cheese.

Return baking sheet with pan to oven and continue baking for 35 – 40 minutes or until a knife inserted in centre comes out clean. Let stand for 10 minutes before serving. Do not freeze.
Serves 8 as an appetizer.

Butter Pastry

   1¼ cups (300 mL) flour
   ½ tsp (2 mL) salt
   ½ cup (125 mL) butter, chilled and cubed
   3 tbsp (40 mL) ice water

Place flour and salt in a food processor; process to combine. Add butter and process, using an on/off motion, until mixture resembles coarse meal. Add ice water and process just until dough starts to come together. Gather dough into a ball; flatten into a disc shape. Wrap disc with plastic wrap and refrigerate for 30 minutes before rolling out.

EGGPLANT

Eggplant is often thought of as a vegetable, but it is actually a fruit. Eggplants come in a variety of colours, shapes and sizes; however, the pear-shaped, deep purple variety is most common. Select eggplants that are smooth, firm and heavy for their size.

BABA GHANOUSH

Baba ghanoush is a purée of eggplant and tahini. It is of Middle Eastern origin and can be served as a dip or a spread with pita bread or flatbread.

1 large eggplant
¼ cup (50 mL) tahini (sesame seed paste)
3 tbsp (40 mL) sour cream
3 tbsp (40 mL) fresh lemon juice
½ tsp (2 mL) salt
Dash freshly ground pepper
3 cloves garlic, crushed
Olive oil, optional

Preheat oven to 400°F (200°C). Pierce eggplant in several places with a fork. Place eggplant in a baking dish.

Bake until tender, about 45 minutes; cool. When cool enough to handle, slice eggplant in half lengthwise and scoop out pulp. Place pulp in a colander and place colander in sink. Let drain for 20 minutes.

Transfer pulp to a food processor; process until smooth. Add next 6 ingredients (tahini through garlic); process, using an on/off motion, until blended. Transfer mixture to a serving dish. Cover and refrigerate for at least 4 hours or up to 24 hours.

To serve, stir mixture and drizzle with oil. Serve with pita bread wedges. *Makes about 1⅓ cups (325 mL).*

CHEESEBURGER MEATBALLS

Our Signature Thousand Island Dressing (recipe on page 54) makes a great dip for these cheese-stuffed meatballs.

½ cup (125 mL) coarse dry bread crumbs or panko
    (Japanese-style bread crumbs)
2 tbsp (25 mL) milk
1 tsp (5 mL) Worcestershire sauce
3 oz (90 g) cheddar cheese
1 lb (0.5 kg) lean ground beef
½ cup (125 mL) finely chopped cooked bacon
1 tsp (5 mL) onion powder
½ tsp (2 mL) dry mustard
½ tsp (2 mL) garlic powder
½ tsp (2 mL) salt
¼ tsp (1 mL) freshly ground pepper
Dill pickle slices

Preheat oven to 375°F (190°C). Line a rimmed baking sheet with nonstick foil.

Combine bread crumbs, milk and Worcestershire sauce. Let stand for 2 minutes. Meanwhile, cut cheese into ½ inch (1.25 cm) cubes. There should be about 32 cubes; set aside.

Combine bread crumb mixture and next 7 ingredients (beef through pepper) until well blended. Shape 1 tbsp (15 mL) measures of beef mixture into balls. Press a small well in centre of each ball. Place a cube of cheese in each well. Wrap beef around cheese and reshape into a ball. Place meatballs in prepared pan.

Bake for 12 – 15 minutes or until completely cooked. Top each meatball with a piece of dill pickle and secure with a toothpick. *Makes about 32.*

FOOD SAFETY FOR GROUND MEAT

Ground meat requires careful handling as it is especially vulnerable to bacterial contamination. All ground meat must be thoroughly cooked in order to destroy harmful bacteria that may be present.

EASY DECORATING TIP

Wrap throw pillows with festive ribbon so that they look like gift packages. Set them along the top of a couch or a comfortable chair.

SMOKED GOUDA AND CARAMELIZED ONION QUESADILLAS

2 tbsp (25 mL) butter
2 cups (500 mL) thinly sliced onions
1 tbsp (15 mL) packed brown sugar
¼ tsp (1 mL) raspberry or red wine vinegar
1½ cups (375 mL) shredded smoked Gouda cheese
8 flour tortillas (8 inch/20 cm)
Freshly ground pepper
1 tbsp (15 mL) butter

Melt 2 tbsp (25 mL) butter in a medium frypan over low heat. Add onions, brown sugar and vinegar; cook, stirring frequently, until onions are golden brown, about 25 minutes. Remove from heat and cool completely.

Preheat oven to 350°F (180°C). Combine onion mixture and cheese in a bowl. Spread mixture evenly over one side of 4 tortillas, leaving a ¼ inch (6 mm) border. Sprinkle with pepper. Cover with remaining 4 tortillas.

Melt 1 tsp (5 mL) butter in a medium frypan. Cook quesadillas, one at a time, adding remaining butter as necessary, until lightly browned, about 2 minutes per side. Transfer quesadillas to cookie sheets.

Bake for 5 minutes or until heated through. Cut into wedges. *Serves 6 – 8.*

Soups

Cabbage Soup with Garlic Sausage (page 40)

CABBAGE SOUP WITH GARLIC SAUSAGE

1 tbsp (15 mL) oil
1 ring (300 g) garlic sausage, halved lengthwise and sliced crosswise
  (¼ inch/6 mm)
1 cup (250 mL) chopped onion
½ tsp (2 mL) salt
½ tsp (2 mL) freshly ground pepper
4 cups (1 L) chopped green cabbage
1 tbsp (15 mL) whole grain mustard
6 cups (1.5 L) chicken broth
2 cups (500 mL) cubed unpeeled red potatoes (½ inch/1.25 cm)
2 tbsp (25 mL) white wine vinegar
4 cups (1 L) coarsely chopped fresh spinach

Heat oil in a Dutch oven over medium heat. Add sausage and cook, stirring, until browned, about 5 minutes. Transfer sausage to a bowl; set aside.

Add onion, salt and pepper to pan; sauté until onion is softened, about 5 minutes. Add cabbage and mustard; cook, stirring, until cabbage starts to soften, about 3 – 5 minutes.

Return sausage to pan. Stir in broth, potatoes and vinegar. Bring to a boil. Reduce heat and simmer, covered, stirring occasionally, until cabbage and potatoes are tender, about 20 minutes. Add spinach and cook, stirring, until spinach wilts. This soup does not freeze well. *Serves 6 – 8.*

Ukrainian Beet Soup

6 slices bacon, chopped
1 cup (250 mL) finely chopped onion
½ cup (125 mL) diced celery
4 cloves garlic, finely chopped
3 cups (750 mL) beef broth
3 cups (750 mL) chicken broth
3 cups (750 mL) julienned peeled beets
2 cups (500 mL) sliced carrots
4 stalks fresh dill or 1 tsp (5 mL) dried dill weed
2 cups (500 mL) cubed peeled yellow potatoes (½ inch/1.25 cm)
2 cups (500 mL) chopped green cabbage
2 tbsp (25 mL) fresh lemon juice
2 tbsp (25 mL) white wine vinegar
1 tsp (5 mL) grated lemon peel
Salt and freshly ground pepper
Sour cream
Chopped fresh dill

Cook bacon in a Dutch oven over medium heat until browned and crisp. Remove from heat.

Remove bacon with a slotted spoon; drain bacon on paper towels. Drain off all but 2 tbsp (25 mL) fat from pan. Return pan to medium heat. Add onion and celery; sauté, scraping to loosen browned bits, until vegetables are softened, about 5 minutes. Add garlic and sauté for 1 minute. Stir in beef broth, chicken broth, beets, carrots and dill stalks. Bring to a boil. Reduce heat and simmer, covered, stirring occasionally, for 10 minutes.

Return bacon to pan. Add potatoes and cabbage; cook, covered, stirring occasionally, until potatoes and cabbage are tender, about 10 minutes. Remove from heat.

Remove and discard dill stalks. Stir in lemon juice, vinegar and lemon peel. Season to taste with salt and pepper. Ladle into bowls. Top with sour cream and chopped dill. This soup does not freeze well. *Serves 6 – 8.*

Did You Know?

Beets can transfer their red colour to your hands and work surfaces. ATCO Blue Flame Kitchen recommends wearing disposable gloves when peeling and slicing beets.

CARROT AND TARRAGON BISQUE

This rich soup makes a great appetizer at a small dinner party.

¼ cup (50 mL) butter
1 cup (250 mL) diced onion
2 cups (500 mL) shredded carrots
2 cups (500 mL) chicken broth
1 tbsp (15 mL) chopped fresh tarragon or 1 tsp (5 mL) dried tarragon, crumbled
1 tbsp (15 mL) fresh lemon juice
½ tsp (2 mL) grated lemon peel
¼ tsp (1 mL) salt
⅛ tsp (0.5 mL) freshly ground pepper
⅛ tsp (0.5 mL) celery seed
½ cup (125 mL) whipping cream

Melt butter in a Dutch oven over medium heat. Add onion and sauté until softened, about 5 minutes. Add carrots and cook, stirring, for 2 minutes. Stir in broth. Bring to a boil. Reduce heat and simmer, covered, stirring occasionally, until carrots are tender, about 10 minutes. Remove from heat.

Purée mixture in a blender. May be prepared to this point, cooled quickly and refrigerated for up to 24 hours. To cool quickly, transfer mixture to shallow containers and stir frequently.

Return mixture to pan. Stir in next 6 ingredients (tarragon through celery seed) and cook over low heat, stirring frequently, until heated through. Remove from heat and stir in cream. Serve immediately.
Serves 4 as a starter.

Carrot and Tarragon Bisque

Yams and Sweet Potatoes

Yams that are sold in North America are actually sweet potatoes. What are referred to as yams in our grocery stores are a soft-fleshed variety of sweet potato that has a bright orange colour and a soft, moist, sugary texture. What are sold as sweet potatoes are lighter in colour with a drier, more mealy texture.

Roasted Sweet Potato and White Chocolate Soup

5 cups (1.25 L) cubed peeled sweet potatoes (1 inch/2.5 cm)
2 tbsp (25 mL) oil
⅛ tsp (0.5 mL) salt
⅛ tsp (0.5 mL) freshly ground pepper
1 whole vanilla bean
½ cup (125 mL) butter
¾ cup (175 mL) chopped onion
4 cups (1 L) chicken broth
3 squares white chocolate, chopped
½ cup (125 mL) whipping cream
2 tbsp (25 mL) chopped fresh dill
1½ tsp (7 mL) fresh lemon juice

Preheat oven to 400°F (200°C). Line a rimmed baking sheet with parchment paper.

Combine sweet potatoes, oil, salt and pepper in a large bowl; toss until coated. Place sweet potatoes in a single layer in prepared pan.

Bake, uncovered, stirring occasionally, for 35 – 40 minutes or until sweet potatoes are lightly browned; cool.

Cut vanilla bean in half lengthwise and scrape beans from pod; set pod and beans aside.

Melt half of butter in a Dutch oven over medium heat. Add onion and sauté until softened, about 5 minutes. Add remaining butter, sweet potatoes, vanilla bean pod and beans. Stir in broth. Bring to a boil. Reduce heat and simmer, uncovered, stirring occasionally, for 15 – 20 minutes. Remove from heat.

Remove and discard vanilla bean pod. Purée mixture in batches in a blender, filling blender no more than half full for each batch and adding white chocolate to last batch.

Return mixture to pan. Stir in cream. Cook over low heat, stirring frequently, until heated through. Do not boil. Stir in dill and lemon juice. Serve immediately. *Serves 6 as a starter.*

TURKEY MULLIGATAWNY SOUP
Mulligatawny soup originated in India and means "pepper water". It is made with a meat or vegetable stock that is seasoned with curry and other spices.

2 tbsp (25 mL) oil
1 cup (250 mL) chopped onion
1 clove garlic, crushed
2 tbsp (25 mL) curry powder
5 cups (1.25 L) turkey stock
1 can (14 oz/398 mL) diced tomatoes
1 can (10 oz/284 mL) cream of chicken soup
2 medium carrots, diced
2 stalks celery, sliced
½ tsp (2 mL) ground ginger
½ tsp (2 mL) salt
⅛ tsp (0.5 mL) nutmeg
1½ cups (375 mL) diced cooked turkey
2 Golden Delicious apples, peeled and diced
2 cups (500 mL) cooked rice

Heat oil in a Dutch oven over medium heat. Add onion and garlic; sauté for 2 minutes. Add curry powder and cook, stirring, for 1 minute. Stir in next 8 ingredients (stock through nutmeg). Bring to a boil. Reduce heat and add turkey and apples. Simmer, covered, stirring occasionally, for 30 minutes. Stir in rice and cook, stirring, until heated through, about 5 minutes. *Serves 6 – 8.*

SAFETY MATTERS

Never pour water onto a cooking oil fire! This will cause the fire to flare and spread. Instead, turn off the stove and put a lid on the pot to smother the flame.

For more safety tips, visit www.atcogas.com.

SMOKED PAPRIKA

Smoked paprika, also known as pimenton, is made from Spanish red peppers that are dried and smoked over wood planks. This gives smoked paprika its characteristic smoky flavour. If unavailable, regular paprika may be used.

HUNGARIAN GOULASH SOUP

2 lb (1 kg) stewing beef, cubed
Salt and freshly ground pepper
1 cup (250 mL) chopped bacon
2 cups (500 mL) diced onions
3 cloves garlic, finely chopped
3 tbsp (40 mL) paprika
2 tsp (10 mL) caraway seed
½ tsp (2 mL) smoked paprika
6 cups (1.5 L) beef broth
1 can (28 oz/796 mL) diced tomatoes
½ cup (125 mL) diced drained canned roasted red peppers, patted dry
3 tbsp (40 mL) red wine vinegar
3 cups (750 mL) diced unpeeled yellow potatoes (¼ inch/6 mm)
1 cup (250 mL) sour cream

Sprinkle beef with salt and pepper; set aside. Cook bacon in a Dutch oven over medium heat until browned and crisp. Remove from heat.

Remove bacon with a slotted spoon; drain bacon on paper towels. Return pan to medium-high heat. Add beef in batches and brown on all sides. Transfer beef to a plate.

Reduce heat to medium. Add onions and sauté, scraping to loosen browned bits, until softened, about 5 minutes. Add garlic and sauté for 1 minute. Stir in paprika, caraway seed and smoked paprika.

Return bacon, beef and any accumulated juices to pan. Stir in broth, tomatoes, roasted peppers and vinegar. Bring to a boil. Reduce heat and simmer, covered, stirring occasionally, for 1½ – 2 hours or until beef is tender. May be prepared to this point, cooled quickly and refrigerated for up to 24 hours. To cool quickly, transfer mixture to shallow containers and stir frequently.

Bring to a boil before proceeding. Reduce heat to a simmer. Add potatoes and cook, covered, stirring occasionally, until potatoes are tender, about 20 minutes.

Reduce heat to low. Stir in sour cream and cook, stirring frequently, until heated through. Serve immediately. This soup does not freeze well. *Serves 8.*

FENNEL AND LEEK SOUP

2 tbsp (25 mL) butter
¼ cup (50 mL) chopped onion
4 cups (1 L) cubed fennel (½ inch/1.25 cm)
4 cups (1 L) sliced leeks (white and tender light green portions only)
1 cup (250 mL) chopped celery
¼ cup (50 mL) dry sherry
6 cups (1.5 L) chicken broth
3 cups (750 mL) cubed peeled potatoes (½ inch/1.25 cm)
1 can (19 oz/540 mL) white kidney beans, rinsed and drained
1 tbsp (15 mL) thyme, crumbled
Salt and freshly ground pepper

Melt butter in a Dutch oven over medium heat. Add onion and sauté for 1 minute. Add fennel, leeks and celery; sauté until vegetables are softened and lightly browned, about 10 minutes. Add sherry and cook, stirring, until most of liquid has evaporated, about 1 – 2 minutes. Stir in broth and potatoes. Bring to a boil. Reduce heat and simmer, covered, stirring occasionally, for 30 minutes. Remove from heat.

Purée mixture in batches in a blender, filling blender no more than half full for each batch.

Return mixture to pan. Stir in beans and thyme. Cook over medium heat, stirring frequently, until heated through. Season to taste with salt and pepper. *Serves 6 – 8.*

DID YOU KNOW?

Before using leeks, you need to remove the tough outer leaves and trim off the top and root ends. Cut leeks in half lengthwise and wash thoroughly under cool running water to remove any dirt or sand trapped between the leaf layers.

NEW ENGLAND CLAM CHOWDER

When people think of clam chowder, they think of New England clam chowder, also known as Boston clam chowder. It is made with cream or milk.

6 slices thick bacon, julienned
1 cup (250 mL) chopped onion
1 cup (250 mL) chopped celery
2 cans (5 oz/142 g each) whole baby clams
1 can (14 oz/398 mL) clam nectar
1½ cups (375 mL) diced peeled potatoes
½ tsp (2 mL) thyme, crumbled
¼ tsp (1 mL) garlic powder
¼ tsp (1 mL) hot pepper sauce
1 bay leaf
2 cups (500 mL) light cream (10%)
Chopped fresh parsley

Cook bacon in a Dutch oven over medium heat until crisp. Remove from heat.

Remove bacon with a slotted spoon; drain bacon on paper towels. Drain off all but 2 tbsp (25 mL) fat from pan. Return pan to medium heat. Add onion and celery to pan; sauté until softened, about 5 minutes. Drain clams, reserving liquid; set clams aside. Add reserved clam liquid and next 6 ingredients (clam nectar through bay leaf) to onion mixture. Bring to a boil. Reduce heat and simmer, covered, stirring occasionally, until potatoes are tender, about 20 minutes. Stir in bacon, clams and cream. Cook, stirring frequently, just until chowder is heated through. Do not boil. Remove and discard bay leaf. Sprinkle with parsley. *Serves 4 – 6.*

 Cook's Note: *If clam nectar is unavailable, 1¾ cups (425 mL) chicken broth may be used.*

SALADS

Greens with Goat Cheese and Pomegranate Seeds (page 50)

POMEGRANATE SEEDS

To release pomegranate seeds from a pomegranate, first cut off the blossom end of the fruit without piercing the seeds. Using a sharp knife, lightly score the rind into quarters. Holding the pomegranate over a bowl, break pomegranate open on the score lines. Bend back the rind, peel off the cream-coloured membranes and gently push the seeds into the bowl. Depending on its size, one pomegranate will yield about 1⅓ cups (325 mL) seeds. Pomegranate seeds may be refrigerated for up to 2 days or frozen for up to 3 months.

GREENS WITH GOAT CHEESE AND POMEGRANATE SEEDS

¼ cup (50 mL) olive oil
2 tbsp (25 mL) fresh lemon juice
1 tbsp (15 mL) thawed frozen orange juice concentrate
¼ tsp (1 mL) salt
¼ tsp (1 mL) freshly ground pepper
10 cups (2.5 L) torn mixed greens
½ cup (125 mL) pomegranate seeds
⅓ cup (75 mL) thinly sliced red onion
3 medium navel oranges, peeled, sectioned and chopped
1 log (150 g) soft goat cheese, crumbled

To prepare dressing, whisk together oil, lemon juice, orange juice concentrate, salt and pepper until blended.

Combine greens, pomegranate seeds, onion, oranges and cheese in a bowl. Add dressing and toss to coat. Serve immediately. *Serves 8.*

WALDORF APPLE SLAW

½ cup (125 mL) mayonnaise
1 tbsp (15 mL) fresh lemon juice
1 tbsp (15 mL) rice vinegar
2 tsp (10 mL) grated fresh ginger
1 tsp (5 mL) sugar
4 large apples, cut into thin strips
1 cup (250 mL) thinly sliced celery

To prepare dressing, whisk together mayonnaise, lemon juice, vinegar, ginger and sugar until blended.

Combine apples and celery in a bowl. Add dressing and toss to combine. *Serves 8.*

Green Bean Salad with Raspberry Vinaigrette

¼ cup (50 mL) olive oil
1 tbsp (15 mL) raspberry vinegar
1 tsp (5 mL) honey
1 tsp (5 mL) whole grain mustard
½ tsp (2 mL) dry mustard
Dash salt
1 clove garlic, bruised
4 cups (1 L) cut green beans (2 inch/5 cm)
1 red bell pepper, thinly sliced
⅓ cup (75 mL) thinly sliced green onions
¼ cup (50 mL) pine nuts

To prepare raspberry vinaigrette, whisk together first 7 ingredients (oil through garlic) until blended; set aside.

Cook beans in boiling salted water for 1½ minutes; drain. Cool immediately in ice water; drain.

Combine beans, red pepper and green onions in a bowl. Remove and discard garlic from raspberry vinaigrette. Stir raspberry vinaigrette and pour over bean mixture; toss to combine. Sprinkle with pine nuts. *Serves 4.*

 Cook's Note: *To bruise garlic, peel clove and flatten it with a glass or the side of a knife blade.*

Safety Matters

Never let your vehicle run inside the garage, even with the door open. Idling in an enclosed space can put you and your family at risk of carbon monoxide poisoning.

For more safety tips, visit www.atcogas.com.

BRUSSELS SPROUTS SALAD WITH WARM BACON AND PECAN DRESSING

½ lb (0.25 kg) Brussels sprouts
6 cups (1.5 L) torn romaine lettuce
½ cup (125 mL) sliced green onions
1½ cups (375 mL) chopped bacon
½ cup (125 mL) coarsely chopped pecans
¼ cup (50 mL) oil
3 tbsp (40 mL) white wine vinegar
½ tsp (2 mL) whole grain mustard
1 clove garlic, finely chopped
¼ tsp (1 mL) salt
⅛ tsp (0.5 mL) freshly ground pepper

Trim off the ends of stems of Brussels sprouts; discard ends. Cut Brussels sprouts in half lengthwise and then thinly slice crosswise. There should be about 2 cups (500 mL). Combine Brussels sprouts, lettuce and green onions in a bowl; set aside.

To prepare dressing, cook bacon and pecans in a medium frypan over medium heat until bacon is browned and crisp. Remove from heat.

Remove bacon and pecans with a slotted spoon; drain bacon and pecans on paper towels. Drain off all fat from frypan. Return frypan to low heat. Add oil, vinegar, mustard and garlic; cook, scraping to loosen browned bits, for 30 seconds. Return bacon and pecans to frypan. Stir in salt and pepper.

Pour dressing over Brussels sprouts mixture and toss to coat. Serve immediately. *Serves 8.*

Brussels Sprouts Salad with Warm Bacon and Pecan Dressing

LEMONS

When buying lemons, choose fruit that is firm and heavy for its size and has bright colourful skin. The heavier the lemon, the more juice it contains. One medium lemon contains about 3 tbsp (40 mL) juice.

OUR SIGNATURE THOUSAND ISLAND DRESSING

½ cup (125 mL) mayonnaise
¼ cup (50 mL) ketchup
2 tbsp (25 mL) finely chopped red bell pepper
1 hard-cooked egg, peeled and finely chopped
1 tbsp (15 mL) sweet green pickle relish
1 tbsp (15 mL) fresh lemon juice
1 tsp (5 mL) Worcestershire sauce
⅛ tsp (0.5 mL) onion powder
⅛ tsp (0.5 mL) freshly ground pepper
Pinch cayenne pepper

Place all ingredients in a food processor; process until smooth. May be refrigerated for up to 24 hours. Stir before using. *Makes 1¼ cups (300 mL).*

COCOA NIB VINAIGRETTE

Cocoa nibs are pieces of roasted husked cocoa bean. They are used in recipes to provide a crunchy mouth feel and a hint of chocolate taste. Look for cocoa nibs in specialty food stores or specialty chocolate stores.

¼ cup (50 mL) finely chopped shallots
2 tbsp (25 mL) balsamic vinegar
2 tbsp (25 mL) cocoa nibs
1 tbsp (15 mL) chopped fresh tarragon
⅛ tsp (0.5 mL) salt
⅛ tsp (0.5 mL) freshly ground pepper
½ cup (125 mL) grapeseed oil

Place all ingredients except oil in a food processor; process to combine. With machine running, gradually pour oil through feed tube of food processor; process until blended. May be refrigerated for up to 3 days.

Remove vinaigrette from refrigerator and let stand for 30 minutes; stir before using. *Makes ¾ cup (175 mL).*

 Cook's Note: *If desired, 2 tbsp (25 mL) chopped unsweetened chocolate may be substituted for the cocoa nibs in this recipe.*

HOLIDAY SALAD WITH FENNEL

½ cup (125 mL) dried cranberries
½ cup (125 mL) olive oil
2 tbsp (25 mL) balsamic vinegar
2 tbsp (25 mL) white wine vinegar
1 tbsp (15 mL) Dijon mustard
½ tsp (2 mL) sugar
½ tsp (2 mL) salt
½ tsp (2 mL) freshly ground pepper
8 cups (2 L) torn mixed greens
1 medium fennel bulb, trimmed and thinly sliced

Place cranberries in a bowl. Pour enough hot water over cranberries to cover. Let stand for 5 minutes; drain. Set 2 tbsp (25 mL) cranberries aside.

To prepare dressing, place remaining cranberries and next 7 ingredients (oil through pepper) in a blender; purée until smooth. Transfer dressing to a bowl; stir in reserved cranberries.

Combine greens and fennel in a bowl. Add some of the dressing and toss to coat. Serve immediately. Remaining dressing may be refrigerated for up to 2 days. *Serves 8.*

ENERGY MATTERS

A natural gas fireplace can create a separate heating zone in the home allowing the house thermostat to be turned down when only that room is being used.

For more energy saving ideas, visit www.atcoenergysense.com.

MARINATED VEGETABLE SALAD

1 cup (250 mL) oil
½ cup (125 mL) white wine vinegar
⅓ cup (75 mL) pure white vinegar
¼ cup (50 mL) fresh lemon juice
2 tsp (10 mL) salt
1 tsp (5 mL) dry mustard
1 tsp (5 mL) oregano, crumbled
1 tsp (5 mL) sugar
½ tsp (2 mL) celery seed
½ tsp (2 mL) garlic powder
2 cups (500 mL) broccoli florets
2 cups (500 mL) cauliflower florets
2 cups (500 mL) sliced zucchini (½ inch/1.25 cm)
1 can (398 mL) miniature corn, drained and cut into
   1 inch (2.5 cm) pieces
1½ cups (375 mL) halved grape or cherry tomatoes
1½ cups (375 mL) sliced carrots
1½ cups (375 mL) sliced celery
½ cup (125 mL) thinly sliced onion

To prepare dressing, whisk together first 10 ingredients (oil through garlic powder) until blended.

Combine next 8 ingredients (broccoli through onion) in a large bowl. Add dressing and toss to combine. Cover and refrigerate, stirring occasionally, for at least 6 hours or up to 24 hours.

Drain vegetable mixture and transfer to a serving dish; discard dressing.
Serves 8 – 10.

 Cook's Note: *Zucchini should be halved lengthwise and then sliced crosswise before measuring.*

MAINS

Turkey Pot Pie (page 58)

TURKEY POT PIE

¼ cup (50 mL) butter
1 cup (250 mL) diced onion
½ cup (125 mL) diced carrot
½ cup (125 mL) diced celery
2 cups (500 mL) sliced mushrooms
2 cups (500 mL) cubed unpeeled red potatoes
2 cups (500 mL) chicken broth
1 tbsp (15 mL) soy sauce
3 tbsp (40 mL) cornstarch
1 cup (250 mL) milk
2 cups (500 mL) cubed cooked turkey
½ cup (125 mL) frozen green peas, thawed
½ cup (125 mL) plain yogurt
¼ cup (50 mL) chopped fresh parsley
¼ tsp (1 mL) freshly ground pepper
Flour (for dusting surface)
Easy Puff Pastry (recipe on page 59)
1 egg
1 tbsp (15 mL) water

Preheat oven to 350°F (180°C). Melt butter in a large deep frypan over medium heat. Add onion and sauté for 3 minutes. Add carrot and celery; cook, stirring, for 2 minutes. Add mushrooms and cook, stirring, until mushrooms are lightly browned and liquid is evaporated, about 5 minutes. Stir in potatoes, chicken broth and soy sauce. Bring to a boil. Reduce heat and simmer, covered, stirring occasionally, until potatoes are tender, about 15 minutes.

Whisk together cornstarch and milk until blended. Whisk into vegetable mixture. Cook, stirring, until thickened, about 1 minute. Remove from heat.

Stir in turkey, peas, yogurt, parsley and pepper. Spoon into a greased 9x13 inch (23x33 cm) baking dish; set aside. On a floured surface, roll out chilled Easy Puff Pastry ⅛ inch (3 mm) thick. Trim pastry to fit baking dish. Place pastry on top of filling in baking dish. Whisk together egg and water until blended. Brush pastry with egg mixture. Cut large vents in pastry to allow steam to escape.

Bake for 30 – 35 minutes or until pastry is golden brown and filling is bubbly and heated through. Let stand for 5 minutes before serving. *Serves 6 – 8.*

 Cook's Note: *If desired, the filling in this recipe may be divided among heatproof ramekins. Place a round of Easy Puff Pastry on top of filling in each ramekin, cutting large vents in pastry to allow steam to escape. Bake until pastry is golden brown and filling is bubbly and heated through.*

EASY PUFF PASTRY
This dough resembles store-bought puff pastry.

1 cup (250 mL) flour
⅔ cup (150 mL) butter, chilled and cubed
⅓ cup (75 mL) sour cream
Flour

Place flour and butter in a food processor; process, using an on/off motion, until mixture resembles coarse meal. Add sour cream and process, using an on/off motion, just until dough comes together.

Turn dough out onto a floured surface. Using floured hands, shape dough into a rectangle measuring about 8x12 inches (20x30 cm). Place rectangle with long side parallel to edge of work surface. From one short side, fold one-third of dough toward centre. From other short side, fold one-third of dough toward centre, laying it on top. Rotate dough one-quarter turn and roll out into a rectangle measuring about 8x12 inches (20x30 cm). With long side parallel to edge of work surface; repeat folding, rotating and rolling procedure two times, dusting dough with additional flour as needed. With long side parallel to edge of work surface; repeat folding procedure. Wrap folded dough with plastic wrap and refrigerate for 30 minutes before rolling out. *Makes enough dough to top a 9x13 inch (23x33 cm) casserole.*

DID YOU KNOW?

Making puff pastry is an involved process of folding and rolling the dough, resulting in a rich, buttery pastry comprised of many layers that puff when baked.

If chocolate is stored at too low or too high a temperature, a streaking of grey (bloom) can appear on its surface. This is caused by sugar crystals forming or cocoa butter rising to the surface. It does not indicate spoilage.

MOLE CHICKEN

Mole (pronounced MOH-lay) is a traditional Mexican sauce usually served with poultry and meat. It is a smooth cooked blend made from a variety of ingredients including onion, garlic, chiles and, its signature ingredient, chocolate. The chocolate contributes to the dark brown colour and rich flavour of the sauce. Enjoy this dish over hot cooked rice.

1 cup (250 mL) sour cream
½ cup (125 mL) chopped fresh cilantro
12 boneless skinless chicken thighs
Salt and freshly ground pepper
3 tbsp (40 mL) oil
1½ cups (375 mL) chopped green bell peppers
1½ cups (375 mL) chopped onions
3 cloves garlic, finely chopped
1 tbsp (15 mL) finely chopped seeded serrano chile
2 tbsp (25 mL) chili powder
2 tbsp (25 mL) ground cumin
½ tsp (2 mL) cinnamon
2 cups (500 mL) chicken broth, divided
1 can (14 oz/398 mL) fire-roasted diced tomatoes
1 cup (250 mL) dark beer
¼ cup (50 mL) raisins
2 tbsp (25 mL) peanut butter
2 tbsp (25 mL) sugar
1 tsp (5 mL) salt
2 canned chipotle peppers in adobo sauce
2 squares unsweetened chocolate, chopped
1 tsp (5 mL) fresh lime juice

Combine sour cream and cilantro until blended. Cover and refrigerate until serving.

Sprinkle chicken lightly with salt and pepper. Heat oil in a Dutch oven over medium-high heat. Add chicken in batches and brown on both sides. Transfer chicken to a plate.

To prepare sauce, add green peppers, onions, garlic and chile to pan. Cook, stirring, over medium heat until lightly browned, about 5 – 6 minutes. Add chili powder, cumin and cinnamon; cook, stirring, for 3 minutes. Add 1 cup (250 mL) broth. Stir in next 7 ingredients (tomatoes through chipotle peppers). Bring to a boil. Reduce heat and simmer, uncovered, stirring occasionally, until sauce is reduced and thickened, about 20 minutes. Transfer mixture to a blender; purée until smooth. Add chocolate and purée until blended.

Return chicken, any accumulated juices and sauce to pan; stir to combine. Stir in remaining 1 cup (250 mL) broth. Bring to a boil over medium heat. Reduce heat and simmer, covered, stirring frequently, for 45 minutes or until chicken is tender and cooked through. Remove from heat and stir in lime juice. Serve with sour cream mixture. *Serves 6.*

 Cook's Note: *Hot peppers cause severe skin and eye irritation. Wear disposable gloves when handling hot peppers and avoid touching any exposed skin.*

SAFETY MATTERS

Always be prepared for an emergency, regardless of the cause. Have a 72-hour emergency kit ready. Keep items like ready-to-eat and high-energy foods, bottled water, extra clothing and blankets, a flashlight, candles, matches and a battery-operated radio with extra batteries on hand.

For more safety tips, visit www.atcogas.com.

CHICKEN AND SAUSAGE JAMBALAYA

2 tbsp (25 mL) butter
4 boneless skinless chicken breasts, cut into chunks
1 cup (250 mL) chopped onion
1 cup (250 mL) diced green bell pepper
1 cup (250 mL) sliced celery
1 clove garlic, finely chopped
2 cups (500 mL) long grain white rice
1 ring (500 g) ham garlic sausage, sliced ½ inch (1.25 cm) thick
2 cans (10 oz/284 mL each) chicken broth
1 can (14 oz/398 mL) diced tomatoes
½ tsp (2 mL) salt
½ tsp (2 mL) freshly ground pepper
¼ tsp (1 mL) hot pepper sauce
1 bay leaf
½ lb (250 g) frozen raw shrimp, thawed and rinsed
¼ cup (50 mL) chopped fresh parsley

Melt butter in a Dutch oven over medium heat. Add chicken and cook, stirring, until golden brown. Add onion, green pepper, celery and garlic; sauté for 5 minutes. Stir in next 8 ingredients (rice through bay leaf). Bring to a boil. Reduce heat and simmer, covered, stirring occasionally, for 30 minutes or until rice is tender and most of liquid is absorbed. Meanwhile, peel and devein shrimp, leaving tails intact. Pat shrimp dry with paper towels.

Stir shrimp into rice mixture and cook, covered, for 5 minutes or until shrimp are pink and opaque. Remove and discard bay leaf. Sprinkle with parsley. Serve immediately. *Serves 6 – 8.*

Chicken and Artichokes in Phyllo

8 oz (250 g) cream cheese, softened
¼ cup (50 mL) Dijon mustard
½ tsp (2 mL) salt
½ tsp (2 mL) freshly ground pepper
1 can (14 oz/398 mL) artichoke hearts, drained and chopped
½ cup (125 mL) chopped green onions
2 tbsp (25 mL) chopped fresh parsley
16 sheets phyllo pastry
¾ cup (175 mL) butter, melted
8 boneless skinless chicken breasts
2 tbsp (25 mL) freshly grated Parmesan cheese

Using medium speed of an electric mixer, beat together cream cheese, mustard, salt and pepper until smooth. Stir in artichokes, green onions and parsley.

To prepare each phyllo packet, brush a phyllo sheet with some of the melted butter. Lay a second phyllo sheet on top; brush with melted butter. Spread about 2 tbsp (25 mL) cream cheese mixture over each side of 1 chicken breast. Place chicken diagonally on one corner of buttered phyllo. Fold corner of phyllo over chicken. Fold sides of phyllo over chicken; roll up until end of phyllo is reached. Place packet, seam side down, on a greased rimmed baking sheet. Brush packet with melted butter. Repeat procedure with remaining phyllo sheets, melted butter, cream cheese mixture and chicken breasts. Sprinkle packets with Parmesan cheese. May be prepared to this point and refrigerated for up to 4 hours.

Preheat oven to 350°F (180°C). Bake for 55 – 60 minutes or until golden brown and chicken is cooked through. *Serves 8.*

Did you know?

To prevent phyllo from drying out while preparing recipes, keep unused sheets covered with plastic wrap and a damp tea towel. If left uncovered, a sheet of phyllo will dry out in 1 – 2 minutes.

CROWN ROAST OF PORK WITH PUMPERNICKEL AND SAUSAGE STUFFING

1 meaty crown roast of pork (12 ribs)
1 tsp (5 mL) thyme, crumbled
1 tsp (5 mL) salt
1 tsp (5 mL) sugar
½ tsp (2 mL) paprika
½ tsp (2 mL) sage, crumbled
½ tsp (2 mL) freshly ground pepper
2 tbsp (25 mL) olive oil
1 can (10 oz/284 mL) beef broth
1 cup (250 mL) dry white wine
4 tsp (20 mL) cornstarch
2 tbsp (25 mL) brandy
Pumpernickel and Sausage Stuffing (recipe on page 66)

Preheat oven to 425°F (220°C). Place roast, bone side up, on a rack in a roasting pan. Cover tops of bones with foil. Combine next 6 ingredients (thyme through pepper). Stir in oil. Rub thyme mixture evenly over roast. Crumple a piece of foil to form a ball and place in centre of roast.

Roast for 20 minutes. Reduce oven temperature to 325°F (160°C) and continue roasting for 1¾ – 2 hours or until a meat thermometer registers 155°F (68°C). Transfer roast to a platter and cover with foil. Let stand while making gravy. The internal temperature will continue to rise several degrees during standing. The final temperature should be 160°F (71°C).

To prepare gravy, set roasting pan over medium heat. Add broth and wine to pan. Bring to a boil, scraping to loosen browned bits. Boil, stirring frequently, until liquid is reduced by almost half. Stir together cornstarch and brandy until blended. Whisk cornstarch mixture into broth mixture and cook, whisking constantly, until thickened.

Remove foil from bones and foil ball from centre of roast. Fill centre with some of the Pumpernickel and Sausage Stuffing. Serve remaining stuffing separately. Carve roast between bones to separate ribs. Serve with stuffing and gravy. *Serves 12.*

 Cook's Note: *A crown roast of pork is made up of pork ribs turned and tied to resemble a crown. The meat is frenched, meaning it is cut away from each rib chop so that part of the bone is exposed to form a crown. They are not readily available in regular grocery stores. Ask for them at specialty butcher shops.*

Crown Roast of Pork with Pumpernickel and Sausage Stuffing

PUMPERNICKEL AND SAUSAGE STUFFING

1 lb (500 g) mild Italian sausages, casings removed
2 cups (500 mL) chopped onions
2 cups (500 mL) sliced celery
1 clove garlic, crushed
8 cups (2 L) crustless pumpernickel bread cubes, toasted (¾ inch/2 cm)
2 cups (500 mL) diced peeled Granny Smith apples
1 cup (250 mL) golden raisins
⅓ cup (75 mL) chopped fresh parsley
1 tsp (5 mL) fennel seed, crushed
1 tsp (5 mL) sage, crumbled
½ tsp (2 mL) salt
½ tsp (2 mL) freshly ground pepper
¼ tsp (1 mL) ground allspice
⅛ tsp (0.5 mL) nutmeg
3 eggs
1¼ cups (300 mL) chicken broth

Preheat oven to 325°F (160°C). Place sausages in a large frypan over medium-high heat. Cook, stirring to break up sausages, until browned, about 5 minutes. Reduce heat to medium. Add onions, celery and garlic; sauté until softened, about 5 minutes. Remove from heat.

Combine sausage mixture and next 10 ingredients (bread cubes through nutmeg) in a large bowl. Whisk together eggs and broth. Add to bread cube mixture and stir until combined. Spoon mixture into a greased 9x13 inch (23x33 cm) baking dish.

Bake, uncovered, stirring once, for 60 minutes or until heated through. *Serves 10 – 12.*

 Cook's Note: *To toast bread cubes, preheat oven to 300°F (150°C). Place bread cubes in a single layer on two rimmed baking sheets. Bake for 20 minutes or until dry.*

Turkey Tetrazzini

Tetrazzini is said to have been created in the early 1900s for Italian opera singer Luisa Tetrazzini. The dish became popular for entertaining during the 1950s.

½ cup (125 mL) fine dry bread crumbs
2 tbsp (25 mL) butter, melted
3 tbsp (40 mL) butter
2 cups (500 mL) sliced mushrooms
⅓ cup (75 mL) sliced green onions
3 tbsp (40 mL) flour
2 cups (500 mL) turkey stock or chicken broth
1 cup (250 mL) light cream (10%)
2 tbsp (25 mL) dry sherry
½ tsp (2 mL) freshly ground pepper
¼ tsp (1 mL) salt
Dash nutmeg
½ cup (125 mL) freshly grated Parmesan cheese, divided
4 cups (1 L) cubed cooked turkey
16 oz (500 g) spaghetti, cooked, rinsed and drained
½ cup (125 mL) diced drained canned roasted red peppers

Preheat oven to 350°F (180°C). Combine bread crumbs and 2 tbsp (25 mL) melted butter; set aside.

Melt 3 tbsp (40 mL) butter in a Dutch oven over medium heat. Add mushrooms and green onions; sauté until tender, about 5 minutes. Stir in flour until blended. Gradually stir in stock. Bring to a boil, stirring frequently. Reduce heat and simmer, stirring frequently, until thickened. Stir in cream, sherry, pepper, salt and nutmeg. Add ¼ cup (50 mL) Parmesan cheese and cook, stirring, for 2 minutes. Stir in turkey, cooked spaghetti and roasted peppers.

Transfer mixture to a greased 9x13 inch (23x33 cm) baking dish. Sprinkle with bread crumb mixture and remaining ¼ cup (50 mL) Parmesan cheese.

Bake, uncovered, for 30 minutes or until bubbly and heated through.
Serves 8.

Fine Dry Bread Crumbs

Fine dry bread crumbs can be purchased in grocery stores. To make homemade fine dry bread crumbs, place a single layer of bread slices on a rimmed baking sheet and bake at 300°F (150°C) until completely dry and lightly browned; cool. Process in a food processor until very fine crumbs form.

OSSO BUCO

2 tbsp (25 mL) butter
1½ cups (375 mL) chopped onions
1 cup (250 mL) chopped celery
⅔ cup (150 mL) chopped carrot
2 strips lemon peel (3x½ inch/7.5x1.25 cm)
1 clove garlic, crushed
½ cup (125 mL) flour
8 meaty veal shanks, 1 inch (2.5 cm) thick
3 tbsp (40 mL) olive oil
1 cup (250 mL) dry white wine
1 can (28 oz/796 mL) diced tomatoes
1 tsp (5 mL) salt
¼ tsp (1 mL) freshly ground pepper
¼ tsp (1 mL) basil, crumbled
¼ tsp (1 mL) thyme, crumbled
3 sprigs fresh parsley
2 bay leaves
3 tbsp (40 mL) chopped fresh parsley
1 tbsp (15 mL) grated lemon peel
2 cloves garlic, finely chopped

Melt butter in an ovenproof Dutch oven over medium heat. Add onions, celery and carrot; sauté until tender, about 7 minutes. Add strips of lemon peel and crushed garlic; sauté for 1 minute. Transfer onion mixture to a plate; set aside.

Preheat oven to 350°F (180°C). Place flour in a large heavy plastic bag. Working with one veal shank at a time, add veal to flour and toss to coat. Heat 2 tbsp (25 mL) oil in same pan over medium heat. Add veal in batches and brown on all sides, adding remaining oil as necessary. Transfer veal to a plate.

Add wine to same pan and cook for 30 seconds, scraping to loosen browned bits. Stir in next 7 ingredients (tomatoes through bay leaves). Bring to a boil. Remove from heat. Return veal to pan. Top with onion mixture.

Bake, covered, for 2 hours or until veal is tender. Meanwhile, to prepare gremolata, combine 3 tbsp (40 mL) parsley, grated lemon peel and chopped garlic.

Remove and discard parsley sprigs and bay leaves from osso buco. Sprinkle with gremolata. *Serves 6 – 8.*

 Cook's Note: *Veal shanks are not readily available in regular grocery stores. Ask for them at specialty butcher shops.*

MUSTARD AND PARMESAN-CRUSTED PORK TENDERLOIN

½ cup (125 mL) soft fresh bread crumbs
½ cup (125 mL) chopped fresh parsley
⅓ cup (75 mL) freshly grated Parmesan cheese
½ tsp (2 mL) thyme, crumbled
½ tsp (2 mL) salt
¼ tsp (1 mL) freshly ground pepper
¼ cup (50 mL) Dijon mustard
¾ tsp (3 mL) fennel seed, crushed
1 clove garlic, crushed
2 pork tenderloins (1 lb/0.5 kg each)

Preheat oven to 425°F (220°C). Line a rimmed baking sheet with nonstick foil.

Combine first 6 ingredients (bread crumbs through pepper) in a shallow pan; set aside. Combine mustard, fennel seed and garlic. Spread mustard mixture evenly over tenderloins. Roll tenderloins, one at a time, in bread crumb mixture to coat. Place pork in prepared pan.

Bake, uncovered, for 35 – 40 minutes or until a meat thermometer registers 160°F (71°C). Let stand for 5 minutes before slicing. *Serves 6 – 8.*

SAFETY MATTERS

Clear the area around your furnace of combustible materials such as paper, cardboard or paint cans.

For more safety tips, visit www.atcogas.com.

FRESH GINGER

Fresh ginger (gingerroot) must be peeled as it has a tough skin. Look for smooth-skinned roots as wrinkling indicates the ginger is dry and past its prime. Store tightly wrapped in the refrigerator. After peeling, fresh ginger may be grated, diced or frozen whole. Fresh ginger adds a peppery, slightly sweet flavour and a spicy, pungent aroma to dishes.

BANGKOK BEEF RAGOUT

2 tbsp (25 mL) flour
2 tsp (10 mL) ground coriander
1 tsp (5 mL) ground cardamom
1 tsp (5 mL) ground cumin
1 tsp (5 mL) turmeric
1 tsp (5 mL) freshly ground pepper
¼ tsp (1 mL) cayenne pepper
3 lb (1.5 kg) boneless beef chuck steak, cubed
2 tbsp (25 mL) oil
3 cups (750 mL) sliced onions
1 cup (250 mL) sliced red bell pepper
2 tbsp (25 mL) grated fresh ginger
4 cloves garlic, finely chopped
2 cans (10 oz/284 mL each) beef broth
1 can (400 mL) coconut milk
2 tbsp (25 mL) finely chopped lemon grass stalk (white portion only)
   or 2 tsp (10 mL) grated lemon peel
½ tsp (2 mL) salt
1 cinnamon stick
1 bay leaf
2 tbsp (25 mL) chopped fresh cilantro

Preheat oven to 350°F (180°C). Combine first 7 ingredients (flour through cayenne pepper) in a large plastic bag. Add beef to flour mixture and toss to coat.

Heat 1 tbsp (15 mL) oil in an ovenproof Dutch oven over medium heat. Add beef in batches and brown on all sides, adding remaining oil as necessary. Transfer beef to a plate.

Add onions and red pepper to pan; sauté until tender, about 5 minutes. Add ginger and garlic; sauté for 1 minute. Add next 6 ingredients (broth through bay leaf). Bring to a boil, scraping to loosen browned bits. Return beef and any accumulated juices to pan. Cover pan and transfer to oven.

Bake, covered, stirring occasionally, for 1½ – 2 hours or until meat is tender. Remove and discard cinnamon stick and bay leaf. May be prepared to this point, cooled quickly and refrigerated for up to 24 hours. To cool quickly, transfer ragout to shallow containers and stir frequently.

Reheat ragout over medium heat. Stir in cilantro. Serve immediately. *Serves 6 – 8.*

HAM AND APPLE RISOTTO

¼ cup (50 mL) butter, divided
1 cup (250 mL) diced Golden Delicious apple
½ cup (125 mL) chopped onion
1 cup (250 mL) arborio rice
1 cup (250 mL) diced cooked ham
¼ tsp (1 mL) freshly ground pepper
¾ cup (175 mL) apple juice
4 cups (1 L) chicken broth
⅓ cup (75 mL) freshly grated Parmesan cheese
1 tbsp (15 mL) chopped fresh parsley

Melt 2 tbsp (25 mL) butter in a large saucepan over medium heat. Add apple and sauté until golden brown, about 10 minutes. Transfer apple to a bowl; set aside.

Melt remaining 2 tbsp (25 mL) butter in same saucepan. Add onion and sauté until softened, about 4 minutes. Stir in rice, ham and pepper; sauté for 2 minutes. Stir in apple juice and cook, stirring, until apple juice is almost absorbed. Meanwhile, heat broth to simmering.

Add 1 cup (250 mL) hot broth to rice mixture; cook, stirring frequently, until almost all of liquid is absorbed. Add remaining 3 cups (750 mL) hot broth, 1 cup (250 mL) at a time, cooking and stirring constantly until mixture is creamy, rice is tender and most of liquid is absorbed, about 20 – 25 minutes. Remove from heat.

Stir in apple and Parmesan cheese, stirring until cheese is melted. Sprinkle with parsley. Serve immediately. *Serves 4.*

DID YOU KNOW?

Arborio rice is an Italian short grain rice. Due to its high starch content, when cooked, this rice contributes to a dish's creamy texture, making arborio rice ideal for use in risotto and rice pudding.

SHALLOTS

A shallot is a vegetable belonging to the same family as an onion. Shallots can be found in the produce section of most grocery stores. They are smaller than onions and have a mild onion flavour.

BAKED LOBSTER ON THE SHELL

½ cup (125 mL) panko (Japanese-style bread crumbs) or coarse
  dry bread crumbs
2 tbsp (25 mL) butter, melted
1 tbsp (15 mL) chopped fresh chives
¼ tsp (1 mL) paprika
⅛ tsp (0.5 mL) salt
4 frozen lobster tails, thawed (6 oz/175 g each)
2 tbsp (25 mL) butter
¼ cup (50 mL) finely chopped shallots
½ cup (125 mL) finely chopped fennel
2 tbsp (25 mL) dry sherry
½ cup (125 mL) mashed cooked sweet potato
1 tbsp (15 mL) chopped fresh chives
1 tbsp (15 mL) chopped fresh parsley
1 egg yolk
1 tbsp (15 mL) whipping cream
1 tsp (5 mL) whole grain mustard
½ tsp (2 mL) hot pepper sauce
½ tsp (2 mL) salt
¼ tsp (1 mL) freshly ground pepper

To prepare panko topping, combine panko, 2 tbsp (25 mL) melted butter, 1 tbsp (15 mL) chives, paprika and salt in a bowl; set aside.

Using kitchen shears, cut off legs and cut out bottom of each lobster tail shell; discard legs and bottom of shells. Remove lobster meat from shell tops, reserving shell tops. Cut lobster meat into ½ inch (1.25 cm) pieces; set aside. Rinse shell tops; set aside.

Preheat oven to 375°F (190°C). Melt 2 tbsp (25 mL) butter in a large frypan over medium heat. Add shallots and sauté for 2 minutes. Add fennel and cook, stirring, until fennel is tender, about 2 minutes. Add lobster and cook, stirring frequently, for 1 minute. Stir in sherry. Cook, stirring, until most of liquid has evaporated and meat is opaque and completely cooked, about 2 – 3 minutes. Remove from heat.

Combine next 9 ingredients (sweet potato through pepper) in a bowl. Fold in lobster mixture. Place mixture in a mound in each shell top, dividing equally. Top mixture with panko topping. Place filled shells on a rimmed baking sheet lined with foil. Crumple additional pieces of foil and place crumbled foil pieces between shells to keep shells in place.

Bake for 20 – 25 minutes or until mixture is heated through and panko topping is golden brown. Serve immediately. *Serves 4.*

SHRIMP SCAMPI-STYLE

> 1½ lb (750 g) frozen raw shrimp, thawed and rinsed
> ½ cup (125 mL) butter
> 2 tbsp (25 mL) thinly sliced green onion
> 8 cloves garlic, finely chopped
> ½ cup (125 mL) dry white wine
> ¼ cup (50 mL) fresh lemon juice
> 1 tbsp (15 mL) chopped fresh parsley

Peel and devein shrimp, leaving tails intact. Pat shrimp dry with paper towels; set aside.

Melt butter in a large frypan over medium heat. Add green onion and garlic; sauté for 2 minutes. Stir in wine and lemon juice. Bring to a boil. Reduce heat and simmer, uncovered, stirring occasionally, for 4 minutes. Add shrimp and cook, stirring frequently, until shrimp are pink and opaque, about 3 – 4 minutes. Do not overcook. Sprinkle with parsley. Serve immediately. *Serves 6.*

ENERGY MATTERS

Once set, programmable thermostats save energy by automatically reducing the temperature when people are sleeping or out of the house. The longer your house remains at the lower temperature, the more energy you save.

For more energy saving ideas, visit www.atcoenergysense.com.

BEEF TENDERLOIN ROAST WITH MUSHROOM SAUCE

This recipe calls for a large beef tenderloin roast, making it a good entree to serve to a large group.

5 lb (2.3 kg) beef tenderloin roast
Salt and freshly ground pepper
12 carrots or celery stalks
¼ cup (50 mL) oil, divided
2 tbsp (25 mL) Dijon mustard
2 tbsp (25 mL) finely chopped shallot
1 clove garlic, finely chopped
2 cups (500 mL) sliced mushrooms
2 tbsp (25 mL) tomato paste
½ cup (125 mL) butter
½ cup (125 mL) flour
4 cups (1 L) beef broth
1 tbsp (15 mL) balsamic vinegar
1 tbsp (15 mL) soy sauce
¼ tsp (1 mL) freshly ground pepper

Sprinkle beef with salt and pepper. Let stand for 20 minutes. Meanwhile, preheat oven to 400°F (200°C). Leaving space between pieces, place carrots in a single layer in a shallow roasting pan.

Tie roast with butcher's twine. Heat 2 tbsp (25 mL) oil in a large deep nonstick frypan over medium-high heat. Add roast to frypan and brown on all sides. Place roast on top of carrots in pan. Brush roast with mustard, rotating to brush all sides.

Roast for 45 minutes or until a meat thermometer registers 140°F (60°C). Meanwhile, to prepare sauce, heat remaining 2 tbsp (25 mL) oil in same frypan over medium heat. Add shallot and garlic; sauté until softened, about 2 minutes. Add mushrooms and cook, stirring, until mushrooms are lightly browned and liquid is evaporated, about 5 minutes. Stir in tomato paste. Remove from heat; set aside.

Melt butter in a medium nonstick saucepan over medium heat until bubbly. Add flour and cook, stirring, until flour mixture is browned, about 8 – 10 minutes. Remove from heat and cool for 2 minutes.

Add butter mixture to mushroom mixture and stir to combine. Return frypan to medium heat. Add 2 cups (500 mL) broth and cook, stirring, until thickened and smooth, about 3 minutes. Add remaining 2 cups (500 mL) broth and cook, stirring, until smooth, about 8 minutes. Stir in vinegar, soy sauce and ¼ tsp (1 mL) pepper; keep warm.

Transfer roast to a platter and cover with foil. Let stand for 15 minutes before carving. Serve with sauce. *Serves 12 – 14.*

Beef Tenderloin Roast with Mushroom Sauce

PORTOBELLO MUSHROOMS

Portobello mushrooms are fully mature, large cremini mushrooms and can range in diameter from 4 – 6 inches (10 – 15 cm). As the cremini mushroom matures, the gills open and moisture evaporates, creating a dense texture and intense flavour. Portobello mushrooms are often grilled, sautéed or baked.

VEGETARIAN MOUSSAKA

2 large eggplants
1 tbsp (15 mL) salt
¼ cup (50 mL) olive oil
2 portobello mushrooms
1 tbsp (15 mL) olive oil
1½ cups (375 mL) chopped onions
1 cup (250 mL) chopped carrots
1 cup (250 mL) chopped celery
4 cloves garlic, finely chopped
1 can (28 oz/796 mL) crushed tomatoes
¼ cup (50 mL) chopped fresh parsley
1 tsp (5 mL) oregano, crumbled
½ tsp (2 mL) cinnamon
½ cup (125 mL) freshly grated Parmesan cheese, divided
Custard Topping (recipe on page 77)

Slice each eggplant into ½ inch (1.25 cm) thick rounds. Cut each round into quarters. There should be about 12 cups (3 L). Place eggplant in a bowl. Add salt and toss to coat. Transfer eggplant to a tray lined with several layers of paper towels. Let stand for 30 minutes.

Preheat oven to 425°F (220°C). Rinse eggplant with cold water; drain. Pat eggplant dry with paper towels. Combine eggplant and ¼ cup (50 mL) oil in a bowl; toss until eggplant is coated. Place eggplant in a large rimmed baking sheet.

Bake, uncovered, turning once, for 30 minutes. Meanwhile, remove stems from mushrooms; reserve stems. Using a spoon, scoop gills out of mushrooms; discard gills. Cut mushrooms and stems into ½ inch (1.25 cm) cubes; set aside. Remove eggplant from oven; set aside.

Reduce oven temperature to 350°F (180°C). Heat 1 tbsp (15 mL) oil in a Dutch oven over medium heat. Add mushrooms, stems, onions, carrots, celery and garlic; sauté for 10 minutes. Stir in tomatoes, parsley, oregano and cinnamon; cook, stirring, for 5 minutes. Stir in eggplant and ¼ cup (50 mL) Parmesan cheese. Spoon mixture into a greased shallow 3 quart (3 L) baking dish. Pour Custard Topping evenly over top. Sprinkle with remaining ¼ cup (50 mL) Parmesan cheese.

Bake, uncovered, for 45 – 50 minutes or until golden brown and heated through. Baked moussaka may be refrigerated for up to 24 hours. Remove from refrigerator and let stand for 20 – 30 minutes. Reheat, covered, at 350°F (180°C) for 1 hour or until bubbly and heated through. *Serves 8 – 10.*

CUSTARD TOPPING

½ cup (125 mL) butter
½ cup (125 mL) flour
4 cups (1 L) homogenized milk
½ tsp (2 mL) salt
¼ tsp (1 mL) freshly ground pepper
¼ tsp (1 mL) nutmeg
½ cup (125 mL) freshly grated Parmesan cheese
4 egg yolks, beaten

Melt butter in a large saucepan over medium heat. Stir in flour. Gradually whisk in milk. Stir in salt, pepper and nutmeg. Bring to a boil, stirring frequently. Reduce heat and simmer, stirring frequently, until thickened. Stir in Parmesan cheese. Remove from heat.

Gradually whisk 1 cup (250 mL) of hot milk mixture into beaten egg yolks. Gradually whisk egg yolk mixture back into remaining milk mixture in pan. Use immediately to pour on top of unbaked Vegetarian Moussaka.

DID YOU KNOW?

Cheese graters typically have different sizes of holes that are used to transform cheese into either long thin strips (shredded) or very small particles (grated). As a general rule, firm and semi-soft cheeses are shredded and hard cheeses are grated. Examples of firm and semi-soft cheeses that are shredded include cheddar, mozzarella and Swiss. Examples of hard cheeses that are grated include Parmesan and Romano.

Capers are the unopened flower buds of a shrub native to the Mediterranean and parts of Asia. The buds are picked, dried and then pickled in a vinegar brine. Capers are used to add flavour to dishes or as a garnish. Capers come in various sizes.

SALMON WITH CAPER AND TARRAGON CRUST

½ cup (125 mL) fine dry bread crumbs
¼ cup (50 mL) finely chopped fresh parsley
3 tbsp (40 mL) drained capers, finely chopped
3 tbsp (40 mL) butter, melted
2 tsp (10 mL) grated lemon peel
1 tsp (5 mL) tarragon, crumbled
¼ tsp (1 mL) salt
¼ tsp (1 mL) freshly ground pepper
3½ lb (1.75 kg) salmon fillet
Mustard Cream Sauce (recipe follows)

Preheat oven to 425°F (220°C). Line a large rimmed baking sheet with nonstick foil.

Combine first 8 ingredients (bread crumbs through pepper) in a bowl. Place salmon, skin side down, in prepared pan. Pat bread crumb mixture on top of salmon.

Bake, uncovered, for 40 – 45 minutes or until fish flakes easily with a fork. Using foil as an aid, carefully slide salmon onto a serving platter. Serve with Mustard Cream Sauce. *Serves 8 – 10.*

MUSTARD CREAM SAUCE

½ cup (125 mL) sour cream
3 tbsp (40 mL) Dijon mustard
1 tbsp (15 mL) prepared horseradish
2 tsp (10 mL) fresh lemon juice
¼ tsp (1 mL) salt
¼ tsp (1 mL) freshly ground pepper
½ cup (125 mL) whipping cream

Combine first 6 ingredients (sour cream through pepper). Using medium speed of an electric mixer, beat cream until soft peaks form. Add sour cream mixture and beat until blended. Cover and refrigerate for at least 30 minutes or up to 4 hours. *Makes 1⅓ cups (325 mL).*

Big Batch Chili Con Carne

This recipe serves 50 people, making it perfect for a large crowd.

10 lb (5 kg) lean ground beef
4 cups (1 L) chopped onions
¾ cup (175 mL) chili powder
2 tbsp (25 mL) ground cumin
2 tbsp (25 mL) oregano, crumbled
1 tbsp (15 mL) garlic powder
1 tbsp (15 mL) freshly ground pepper
4 cans (28 oz/796 mL each) diced tomatoes
4 cans (14 oz/398 mL each) baked beans
3 cans (19 oz/540 mL each) red kidney beans, rinsed and drained
2 cans (19 oz/540 mL each) black beans, rinsed and drained
2 cans (680 mL each) tomato sauce
4 cups (1 L) water
4 cups (1 L) frozen kernel corn

Preheat oven to 450°F (230°C). Divide beef and onions between two roasting pans.

Bake, uncovered, stirring every 20 minutes to break up beef, for 1 hour. Using a slotted spoon, transfer beef mixture to a stockpot. Add chili powder, cumin, oregano, garlic powder and pepper; stir to combine. Stir in next 6 ingredients (tomatoes through water). Bring to a boil. Reduce heat and simmer, covered, stirring frequently, for 1 hour.

Stir in corn and simmer, uncovered, stirring occasionally, for 10 minutes. If not serving immediately, chili must be transferred to several shallow containers, stirred frequently so it will cool quickly and refrigerated for up to 24 hours. May be frozen. *Serves 50.*

Canned Beans

Canned beans are rinsed to remove excess salt and any starchy liquid. Drain the rinsed beans thoroughly before using in a recipe. Beans that are canned in a sauce, such as baked beans or chili-style beans, are not rinsed before using.

*Generally, in order to bring out
its full flavour, red wine should
be enjoyed at room temperature.
White wine should be served cool.
The sweeter the white wine, the
colder it should be. Blush wine
also tastes better chilled.*

BEEF TENDERLOIN STEAKS WITH BLUE CHEESE CRUST

1 tbsp (15 mL) butter
¼ cup (50 mL) finely chopped red onion
3 cloves garlic, finely chopped
1 can (10 oz/284 mL) beef broth
¾ cup (175 mL) dry red wine
½ tsp (2 mL) thyme, crumbled
¾ cup (175 mL) crumbled blue cheese
⅓ cup (75 mL) soft fresh bread crumbs
1 tbsp (15 mL) chopped fresh parsley
¼ tsp (1 mL) freshly ground pepper
2 tbsp (25 mL) butter
6 thick beef tenderloin steaks
Salt and freshly ground pepper

Melt 1 tbsp (15 mL) butter in a medium frypan over medium heat. Add onion and garlic; sauté for 2 minutes. Add broth, wine and thyme. Bring to a boil. Boil, uncovered, stirring occasionally, until broth mixture is reduced to 1 cup (250 mL), about 20 minutes. Broth mixture may be prepared in advance and refrigerated for up to 24 hours.

Combine cheese, bread crumbs, parsley and ¼ tsp (1 mL) pepper; set aside. Melt 2 tbsp (25 mL) butter in a large heavy frypan over medium heat. Add steaks and cook to desired doneness, about 4 minutes per side for medium rare.

Preheat broiler. Transfer steaks to a broiler pan. Gently press cheese mixture onto top of steaks.

Broil steaks until cheese is melted and lightly browned, about 2 minutes. Transfer steaks to a platter and cover with foil.

To prepare sauce, pour broth mixture into same large frypan. Bring to a boil over medium heat, scraping to loosen browned bits. Boil, uncovered, for 2 minutes. Season to taste with salt and additional pepper. Serve with steak. *Serves 6.*

Rogan Josh

Rogan Josh is an Indian lamb curry dish. Serve it with our Turmeric Rice (recipe on page 88).

¼ cup (50 mL) oil
2 cups (500 mL) diced onions
2 tsp (10 mL) grated fresh ginger
2 cloves garlic, finely chopped
2 lb (1 kg) boneless lamb, cubed
1 can (28 oz/796 mL) diced tomatoes
1 can (19 oz/540 mL) chickpeas, rinsed and drained
½ cup (125 mL) plain yogurt
½ cup (125 mL) water
2 tbsp (25 mL) ground coriander
1 tsp (5 mL) ground cumin
1 tsp (5 mL) paprika
½ tsp (2 mL) cayenne pepper
½ tsp (2 mL) salt
½ tsp (2 mL) freshly ground pepper
¼ tsp (1 mL) turmeric
⅛ tsp (0.5 mL) cinnamon
⅛ tsp (0.5 mL) ground cloves
⅛ tsp (0.5 mL) nutmeg
¼ cup (50 mL) chopped fresh cilantro, optional
2 tbsp (25 mL) fresh lemon juice
1 tsp (5 mL) grated lemon peel

Heat oil in a large deep frypan over medium heat. Add onions and sauté until softened, about 5 minutes. Add ginger and garlic; sauté for 30 seconds. Add lamb and brown on all sides. Stir in next 14 ingredients (tomatoes through nutmeg). Bring to a boil. Reduce heat and simmer, covered, stirring occasionally, for 1 hour.

Uncover and simmer, stirring occasionally, until mixture is thickened, about 15 minutes. Remove from heat. Stir in cilantro, lemon juice and lemon peel. *Serves 6.*

Coriander

Related to the parsley family, coriander is known for both its seeds and its dark green leaves. Coriander seeds are small and yellow-tan in colour with a flavour similar to a combination of lemon, sage and caraway. The seeds are used either whole or ground. Coriander leaves are commonly known as cilantro.

CAYENNE PEPPER

This hot, fiery chile spice was at one time made from the cayenne pepper, but is now more commonly made from a variety of ground dried chile peppers.

MOROCCAN CHICKEN WITH PRESERVED LEMONS

The preserved lemons called for in this recipe require advance preparation; make them at least 7 days before using.

16 wedges of *Preserved Lemons (recipe on page 83)*
¼ cup (50 mL) flour
½ tsp (2 mL) paprika
¼ tsp (1 mL) salt
1½ tsp (7 mL) freshly ground pepper, divided
8 boneless skinless chicken breasts
2 tbsp (25 mL) olive oil, divided
2 cups (500 mL) sliced onions
4 cloves garlic, finely chopped
1¾ cups (425 mL) chicken broth
½ cup (125 mL) dry white wine
1 tsp (5 mL) turmeric
¼ tsp (1 mL) cayenne pepper
1 cup (250 mL) pitted Sicilian olives, halved lengthwise
2 tbsp (25 mL) chopped fresh cilantro

Scoop pulp out of wedges of Preserved Lemons; discard pulp. Slice each piece of lemon peel lengthwise into 3 pieces; set aside.

Combine flour, paprika, salt, and ½ tsp (2 mL) pepper in a large plastic bag. Add chicken to flour mixture and toss to coat. Heat 1 tbsp (15 mL) oil in a Dutch oven over medium heat. Add chicken in batches and brown on both sides. Transfer chicken to a plate.

Add remaining 1 tbsp (15 mL) oil to pan. Add onions and garlic; sauté for 2 minutes. Stir in broth, wine, turmeric, cayenne pepper and remaining 1 tsp (5 mL) pepper. Bring to a boil. Reduce heat and stir in lemon peel and olives. Return chicken and any accumulated juices to pan. Simmer, covered, stirring occasionally, for 30 minutes or until chicken is cooked through. Sprinkle with cilantro. Serve immediately. *Serves 8.*

PRESERVED LEMONS

When using preserved lemons, it is the peel, not the pulp, that is used. Scoop the pulp out of the preserved lemon wedges and discard it. Slice or chop the lemon peel and use it in recipes to add great flavour.

2 lemons
⅓ cup (75 mL) pickling salt
½ cup (125 mL) fresh lemon juice

Cut each lemon lengthwise into 8 wedges. Pack wedges into a glass jar with a tight-fitting lid. Add salt and toss to coat. Pour lemon juice over lemons and salt. Cover jar and shake gently. The salt will not dissolve completely. Let lemons stand at room temperature for 7 days, shaking jar daily to redistribute lemons. Refrigerate for up to 1 month, shaking jar occasionally.
Makes 16 wedges.

COOKED TO PERFECTION

Meat should be cooked to the following internal temperatures unless otherwise specified by recipe.

Beef, Lamb, Veal (roasts, steaks)

Rare	*140°F (60°C)*
Medium	*160°F (71°C)*
Well done	*170°F (77°C)*

Bison (roasts, steaks)

Rare	*135°F (57°C)*
Medium rare	*145°F (63°C)*
Do not cook beyond	*155°F (68°C)*

Pork (roasts, chops)

Medium	*160°F (71°C)*
Well done	*170°F (77°C)*

SAFETY MATTERS

Check your furnace filter once a month and change or clean it when dirty, according to the manufacturer's specifications. Clean filters help to ensure your furnace works as efficiently as possible and help to keep you and your family safe from exposure to carbon monoxide.

For more safety tips, visit www.atcogas.com.

SOUTHWESTERN VEGETABLE BREAD PUDDING

2 tbsp (25 mL) olive oil
2 cups (500 mL) sliced mushrooms
2 cups (500 mL) sliced zucchini
1 cup (250 mL) sliced red onion
1 each green, red and yellow bell pepper, thinly sliced
1 tsp (5 mL) thyme, crumbled
3 cloves garlic, finely chopped
6 eggs
1½ tsp (7 mL) salt
1½ tsp (7 mL) freshly ground pepper
½ cup (125 mL) whipping cream
4 cups (1 L) crustless French bread cubes
2 cups (500 mL) shredded Swiss cheese
8 oz (250 g) cream cheese, chilled and cubed

Heat oil in a large deep frypan over medium heat. Add next 6 ingredients (mushrooms through garlic) and sauté until vegetables are tender, about 10 minutes. Remove from heat and cool completely.

Whisk together eggs, salt and pepper in a large bowl. Whisk in cream until blended. Add bread cubes, Swiss cheese and cream cheese; stir gently to combine. Gently stir in vegetable mixture. Spoon mixture into a greased shallow 3 quart (3 L) baking dish. May be prepared to this point and refrigerated for up to 24 hours.

Remove baking dish from refrigerator and let stand for 20 – 30 minutes. Meanwhile, preheat oven to 350°F (180°C).

Bake, uncovered, for 50 – 55 minutes or until a knife inserted in centre comes out clean. Let stand for 10 minutes before serving. *Serves 8.*

SIDES

Herbed Popovers (page 86)

GARLIC

Garlic is readily available in many forms. A garlic bulb is the whole head. The head is made up of sections called cloves, each enclosed in a papery skin. Dried garlic flakes are pieces of garlic that need reconstituting. Garlic powder is made by grinding dried garlic flakes. Garlic salt is a blend of garlic powder and salt.

HERBED POPOVERS

1 cup (250 mL) flour
1 cup (250 mL) milk
4 eggs, lightly beaten
½ tsp (2 mL) salt
2 tsp (10 mL) dried chives
2 tsp (10 mL) chopped fresh parsley
2 cloves garlic, finely chopped
2 tbsp (25 mL) oil

Preheat oven to 400°F (200°C). Whisk together flour, milk, beaten eggs and salt just until a smooth batter forms. Stir in chives, parsley and garlic; set aside.

Add ½ tsp (2 mL) oil to each of 12 muffin cups. Heat pan in oven for 10 minutes.

Remove pan from oven. Working quickly, carefully pour batter on top of oil in each muffin cup, filling cups half full. Return pan to oven.

Bake for 15 minutes or until golden brown. Reduce oven temperature to 350°F (180°C) and continue baking for 10 minutes or until well risen, browned and crisp. Serve immediately. *Makes 12.*

CORIANDER COUSCOUS

2 tbsp (25 mL) coriander seed, toasted
3 cups (750 mL) chicken broth
2 cups (500 mL) couscous
¼ cup (50 mL) oil
½ cup (125 mL) chopped dried apricots
¼ cup (50 mL) chopped fresh cilantro

Grind coriander seed in a spice mill or coffee grinder; set aside. Bring chicken broth to a boil in a medium saucepan. Stir in ground coriander, couscous and oil. Remove from heat. Let stand, covered, for 5 minutes.

Fluff couscous with a fork. Add apricots and cilantro; stir to combine.
Serve immediately. *Serves 8.*

OVERNIGHT LEMON HERB POTATOES

This delicious potato dish may be prepared in advance or baked right away.

8 cups (2 L) cubed peeled russet potatoes
3 tbsp (40 mL) butter
¾ cup (175 mL) sour cream
⅓ cup (75 mL) thinly sliced green onions
2 tbsp (25 mL) chopped fresh parsley
1 tbsp (15 mL) fresh lemon juice
1 tsp (5 mL) grated lemon peel
1 tsp (5 mL) thyme, crumbled
1 tsp (5 mL) salt
¼ tsp (1 mL) cayenne pepper
Paprika

Cook potatoes in boiling salted water until tender; drain. Add butter and
mash with a potato masher until smooth. Stir in next 8 ingredients (sour
cream through cayenne pepper). Spoon potato mixture into a greased
shallow 2 quart (2 L) baking dish. Sprinkle with paprika. May be prepared
to this point and refrigerated for up to 24 hours.

Remove baking dish from refrigerator and let stand for 20 – 30 minutes.
Meanwhile, preheat oven to 350°F (180°C).

Bake, covered, for 25 minutes. Uncover and continue baking for 20 minutes
or until potato mixture is heated through. *Serves 8.*

Almonds can be purchased either unblanched (with skins) or blanched (without skins). They are available whole, sliced, slivered, chopped or ground. Unblanched almonds are sometimes labelled natural almonds. In ATCO Blue Flame Kitchen recipes calling for natural almonds, choose unblanched almonds. If a recipe simply calls for almonds, choose blanched almonds.

TURMERIC RICE

¼ cup (50 mL) butter
¾ cup (175 mL) finely chopped onion
1 tsp (5 mL) grated fresh ginger
2 cloves garlic, finely chopped
1½ cups (375 mL) long grain white rice
1 tbsp (15 mL) turmeric
½ tsp (2 mL) salt
2½ cups (625 mL) chicken broth
⅓ cup (75 mL) dried currants
⅓ cup (75 mL) slivered almonds, toasted
¼ cup (50 mL) chopped fresh cilantro

Melt butter in a large saucepan over medium heat. Add onion, ginger and garlic; sauté for 3 minutes. Add rice, turmeric and salt; cook, stirring, for 3 minutes. Stir in broth. Bring to a boil. Reduce heat and simmer, covered, for 20 – 25 minutes, or until liquid is absorbed and rice is tender. Remove from heat. Let stand, covered, for 10 minutes.

Fluff rice with a fork. Stir in currants, almonds and cilantro. *Serves 6.*

CHERRY TOMATO CRUMBLE

1 cup (250 mL) soft fresh bread crumbs
¼ cup (50 mL) freshly grated Parmesan cheese
2 tbsp (25 mL) chopped fresh parsley
1 tbsp (15 mL) olive oil
¼ tsp (1 mL) garlic powder
¼ tsp (1 mL) each salt and freshly ground pepper
5 cups (1.25 L) cherry tomatoes

Preheat oven to 350°F (180°C). Combine all ingredients except tomatoes in a small bowl.

Place tomatoes in a single layer in an ungreased 7½ x11 inch (19x28 cm) baking dish. Sprinkle bread crumb mixture over tomatoes.

Bake for 25 – 30 minutes or until tomatoes are heated through and bread crumb mixture is light golden. Do not overcook as tomatoes will split. *Serves 8.*

POTATO PARSNIP MASH WITH ROASTED GARLIC

6 cups (1.5 L) cubed peeled russet potatoes (1 inch/2.5 cm)
3 cups (750 mL) cubed parsnips (½ inch/1.25 cm)
Mashed garlic pulp from 1 head roasted garlic
½ cup (125 mL) milk, heated
¼ cup (50 mL) butter
¾ tsp (3 mL) salt
⅛ tsp (0.5 mL) freshly ground pepper

Cook potatoes and parsnips in boiling salted water until tender; drain. Add garlic pulp, heated milk, butter, salt and pepper. Mash with a potato masher until smooth. *Serves 8 – 10.*

 Cook's Note: To prepare the roasted garlic for this recipe, preheat oven to 350ºF (180ºC). Cut the top ¼ inch (6 mm) off 1 whole head of garlic. Place head on a piece of foil. Drizzle head with a little olive oil. Twist foil around head to enclose completely. Bake until soft, about 30 – 45 minutes. Squeeze softened garlic out of skins and mash with a fork. One whole head of roasted garlic yields about 2 tbsp (25 mL) mashed garlic pulp. Roasted garlic pulp may be frozen for up to 1 month.

PARSNIPS

Parsnips are root vegetables that resemble white carrots. They can be found in grocery stores throughout the year, but taste best in the fall and winter months as they become sweeter after the first frost.

*Leftover roasted vegetables
may be used in many ways.
Combine roasted vegetables with
cooked couscous, rice, quinoa
or barley and additional seasonings
for a quick pilaf. Heat beef,
chicken or vegetable broth with
cooked rice and roasted vegetables
for an easy and hearty soup.*

ROASTED VEGETABLE MÉLANGE WITH FETA DRESSING

2 Japanese eggplants, diagonally sliced ½ inch (1.25 cm) thick
2 medium zucchini, diagonally sliced ½ inch (1.25 cm) thick
2 red bell peppers, each cut lengthwise into 8 strips
4 Roma tomatoes, each cut into 4 wedges
½ tsp (2 mL) rosemary, crumbled
1 clove garlic, finely chopped
¼ cup (50 mL) olive oil
Feta Dressing (recipe follows)

Preheat oven to 425°F (220°C). Grease a large rimmed baking sheet or line with nonstick foil.

Combine first 6 ingredients (eggplants through garlic) in a large bowl. Add oil and toss until vegetables are coated. Place vegetable mixture in a single layer in prepared pan.

Bake, uncovered, stirring occasionally, for 45 – 50 minutes or until vegetables are tender and lightly browned. Cool to room temperature. Serve with Feta Dressing. *Serves 8.*

FETA DRESSING

1¼ cups (300 mL) shredded feta cheese
½ cup (125 mL) milk
¼ cup (50 mL) olive oil
½ tsp (2 mL) freshly ground pepper
2 cloves garlic, coarsely chopped

Place all ingredients in a blender; purée until smooth. Cover and refrigerate for at least 2 hours or up to 24 hours. *Makes 1⅓ cups (325 mL).*

ASIAN BROCCOLINI

½ cup (125 mL) vegetable broth
¼ cup (50 mL) oyster sauce
1 tbsp (15 mL) cornstarch
2 tsp (10 mL) soy sauce
2 tsp (10 mL) Sriracha sauce
1 tsp (5 mL) sesame oil
1 tsp (5 mL) sugar
3 tbsp (40 mL) oil
2 cups (500 mL) sliced shitake mushrooms
2 cups (500 mL) bean sprouts
1 tsp (5 mL) finely chopped fresh ginger
2 cloves garlic, finely chopped
1 lb (500 g) broccolini, trimmed

To prepare sauce, whisk together first 7 ingredients (broth through sugar) until blended; set aside.

Heat 3 tbsp (40 mL) oil in a large nonstick frypan over medium heat. Add mushrooms and sauté until softened, about 5 minutes. Add bean sprouts, ginger and garlic; cook, stirring, for 2 minutes. Add broccolini and sauté for 3 minutes. Pour sauce over broccolini mixture and stir gently to coat. Cook, uncovered, stirring occasionally, until broccolini is tender, about 3 minutes. *Serves 6 – 8.*

 Cook's Note: *Sriracha sauce, originating in Thailand, is the generic name for a hot and spicy-sweet chili sauce. It is made from dried chili peppers, vinegar, garlic, sugar and salt.*

Broccolini, sometimes called baby broccoli, is a tender and sweet-tasting cross between broccoli and Chinese kale. It is bright green with long, slender stalks and a head of tiny buds that resemble a miniature broccoli head.

DID YOU KNOW?

Oyster sauce is usually found in recipes that have an Asian influence. It is used as a condiment or flavouring agent for meat, poultry, shellfish and vegetable dishes. Oyster sauce is a thick, dark brown, richly flavoured sauce made from oysters, soy sauce, salt and spices. It should be stored in the refrigerator.

YAM BRÛLÉE

    10 cups (2.5 L) cubed peeled yams
    ¾ cup (175 mL) homogenized milk
    ¼ cup (50 mL) butter, cubed
    ¾ tsp (3 mL) cinnamon
    ¾ tsp (3 mL) salt
    ¼ tsp (1 mL) cayenne pepper
    ¼ tsp (1 mL) nutmeg
    ½ cup (125 mL) packed golden brown sugar

Cook yams in boiling salted water until tender, about 20 minutes; drain.

Working in batches, place yams in a food processor; process until smooth. Transfer yams to a bowl. Stir in next 6 ingredients (milk through nutmeg), stirring until butter is melted. Spoon yam mixture into a greased 2 quart (2 L) baking dish. May be prepared to this point and refrigerated for up to 24 hours.

Remove baking dish from refrigerator and let stand for 20 – 30 minutes. Meanwhile, preheat oven to 350°F (180°C).

Bake, covered, for 30 minutes or until heated through. Remove baking dish from oven. Uncover and sprinkle brown sugar on top of yam mixture.

Preheat broiler. Broil until brown sugar is melted and bubbly, about 4 – 5 minutes. *Serves 8 – 10.*

ORANGE MINTED PEAS

    4 cups (1 L) frozen green peas
    ¼ cup (50 mL) sliced green onion
    2 tbsp (25 mL) chopped fresh mint
    1 tbsp (15 mL) butter
    1 tsp (5 mL) grated orange peel
    ¼ tsp (1 mL) salt
    ¼ tsp (1 mL) freshly ground pepper
    ⅛ tsp (0.5 mL) garlic powder

Cook peas in boiling water until tender, about 4 minutes; drain. Place peas in a bowl. Add remaining ingredients (green onion through garlic powder) and stir until combined. *Serves 6 – 8.*

Yam Brûlée

Purchase only clean, uncracked, refrigerated eggs and use them by the best-before date printed on the egg carton. Store eggs in their original carton in the coldest section of the refrigerator; do not store them on the door. Never wash eggs before refrigerating as this removes their protective coating. Thoroughly wash hands, utensils and work surfaces before, during and after egg preparation.

BEET RAVIOLI

Impress your guests with this interesting ravioli made with homemade pasta. Serve these ravioli with your favourite pasta sauce or drizzle them with melted butter.

2 medium beets, trimmed, unpeeled
⅔ cup (150 mL) crumbled feta cheese
3 tbsp (40 mL) chopped toasted walnuts
2 tbsp (25 mL) fine dry bread crumbs
1 tsp (5 mL) grated orange peel
½ tsp (2 mL) salt
¼ tsp (1 mL) freshly ground pepper
⅛ tsp (0.5 mL) celery seed
Fresh Pasta (recipe on page 95)
Flour (for dusting pasta dough and tray)
1 egg
1 tbsp (15 mL) milk

Preheat oven to 400°F (200°C). Wrap beets tightly in foil and place in a baking dish.

Bake until tender when pierced with a fork, about 60 – 75 minutes. Unwrap beets; when cool enough to handle, peel beets and shred. There should be about ⅔ cup (150 mL).

To prepare filling, place beets and next 7 ingredients (cheese through celery seed) in a food processor. Process, using an on/off motion, until almost smooth. Transfer filling to a bowl; set aside.

Divide chilled Fresh Pasta into four pieces; cover three pieces with plastic wrap to prevent them from drying out. Feed remaining piece through a pasta machine according to manufacturer's instructions to form a long thin strip; dusting dough with flour with each pass through the pasta machine. Alternatively, roll piece as thinly as possible on a floured surface into a long thin strip.

Trim strip so that it is about 4 inches (10 cm) wide. Place strip with long side parallel to edge of work surface. Cut strip in half lengthwise; set top

94

half of strip aside. On bottom half of strip, place 1 tsp (5 mL) mounds of filling 1 inch (2.5 cm) apart on centre of strip. Whisk together egg and milk until blended. Lightly brush edges of strip and in between mounds with egg mixture. Place top strip on bottom strip, making edges of dough meet. Press down on edges of dough and in between mounds to squeeze out air and seal. Using a sharp knife, cut in between mounds to make ravioli. Transfer ravioli to a lightly floured tray; cover and set aside. Repeat procedure three times with remaining pieces of dough, filling and egg mixture. Ravioli may be prepared to this point and frozen. If freezing, place ravioli in a single layer on a lightly floured tray; cover and freeze. Once ravioli are frozen, transfer ravioli to an airtight container and freeze for up to 1 month.

If frozen, do not thaw ravioli before cooking. Working in batches, cook ravioli in boiling salted water until ravioli float to surface and dough is tender, about 5 minutes if fresh and 8 – 9 minutes if frozen. *Makes about 48.*

Fresh Pasta

> 4 eggs
> 1 tbsp (15 mL) water
> 1 tsp (5 mL) olive oil
> 2 cups (500 mL) flour
> 1 tsp (5 mL) salt
> Flour, optional

Whisk together eggs, water and oil until blended. Place 2 cups (500 mL) flour and salt in a food processor; process to combine. Add egg mixture and process, using an on/off motion, just until dough comes together, about 30 seconds.

Turn dough out onto a floured surface. If dough is too sticky, gradually knead in additional flour. Gather dough into a ball; flatten into a disc shape. Wrap disc with plastic wrap and refrigerate for at least 30 minutes or up to 8 hours. Roll out using a pasta machine according to manufacturer's instructions or roll out by hand. *Makes about 16 oz (500 g).*

Pasta Primer

Use ample water for cooking pasta. Add salt to water, if desired. Salt will enhance the flavour. Do not add oil to water as it makes pasta slippery and sauce will not cling. Bring water to a boil, add pasta and stir until water returns to a boil. Cook pasta, uncovered, stirring occasionally. Cook just until al dente (tender but firm). Do not overcook. If pasta is to be served with sauce, do not rinse after draining. Serve pasta the moment it is done. Preheating the serving dish will help keep pasta hot.

Are your floors cold? Don't turn up the heat, throw down a rug! Rugs not only help to insulate your floors, especially above unheated spaces such as garages or crawlspaces, but also insulate against noise, helping to make your house quieter.

For more energy saving ideas, visit www.atcoenergysense.com.

QUINOA PILAF WITH VEGETABLES

2 tbsp (25 mL) oil
1 cup (250 mL) quinoa, thoroughly rinsed and drained
½ cup (125 mL) diced celery
½ cup (125 mL) diced red bell pepper
½ cup (125 mL) shredded carrot
¼ cup (50 mL) finely chopped shallots
1½ cups (375 mL) chicken broth
¼ tsp (1 mL) freshly ground pepper
¼ cup (50 mL) toasted pine nuts
2 tbsp (25 mL) thinly sliced green onion
2 tbsp (25 mL) chopped fresh parsley
1 tbsp (15 mL) fresh lemon juice
1 tsp (5 mL) grated lemon peel

Heat oil in a large saucepan over medium heat. Add quinoa and cook, stirring frequently, until quinoa is lightly toasted and fragrant, about 5 minutes. Add celery, red pepper, carrot and shallots; sauté for 3 minutes. Stir in broth and pepper. Bring to a boil. Reduce heat and simmer, covered, until liquid is absorbed and quinoa is tender, about 20 – 25 minutes. Remove from heat. Let stand, covered, for 10 minutes.

Fluff quinoa with a fork. Stir in pine nuts, green onion, parsley, lemon juice and lemon peel. Serve immediately. *Serves 4 – 6.*

BEVERAGES

Gingerbread Eggnog (page 98), Spicy Gingerbread Men (page 118)

FANCY MOLASSES

Fancy molasses is lighter in colour than other kinds of molasses and is more mild and sweet in flavour. It is used in baking or as a topping for foods such as cereals, breads and pancakes. If fancy molasses is called for in a recipe, it is best not to substitute with cooking or blackstrap molasses.

GINGERBREAD EGGNOG

1 cup (250 mL) milk
½ cup (125 mL) light cream (10%)
½ cup (125 mL) pasteurized liquid egg product
2 tbsp (25 mL) fancy molasses
1 tbsp (15 mL) packed golden brown sugar
½ tsp (2 mL) vanilla
¼ tsp (1 mL) cinnamon
¼ tsp (1 mL) ground ginger
Pinch nutmeg
Pinch ground cloves
Whipped cream, optional
Cinnamon, optional

Place first 10 ingredients (milk through cloves) in a blender; blend until thoroughly combined. Refrigerate for at least 30 minutes but no longer than 24 hours.

Stir before serving. Top each serving with a dollop of whipped cream and sprinkle with additional cinnamon. *Serves 2 – 3.*

 Cook's Note: *In recipes where the egg remains uncooked or lightly cooked, it is recommended that pasteurized egg products be used. Pasteurized egg products, such as liquid whole egg and liquid egg white, are available in the refrigerator or freezer section of most grocery stores. ATCO Blue Flame Kitchen used Burnbrae Farms Naturegg Break-Free Liquid Egg Product in this recipe.*

SNOWBALLS

A snowball is a cocktail traditionally made with advocaat, lemonade and sometimes lime juice.

2 cups (500 mL) carbonated lemon-lime beverage, chilled
1⅓ cups (325 mL) lemonade, chilled
¾ cup (175 mL) advocaat (egg liqueur)
¼ cup (50 mL) citrus-flavoured vodka
1½ tbsp (22 mL) fresh lime juice
Ice cubes

Combine lemon-lime beverage, lemonade, advocaat, citrus-flavoured vodka and lime juice in a pitcher. Serve over ice cubes. *Serves 4.*

CRANBERRY MIMOSAS

1 cup (250 mL) cranberry cocktail, chilled
¼ cup (50 mL) Cointreau or other orange liqueur
1 bottle (750 mL) champagne or sparkling white wine, chilled

Combine cranberry cocktail and Cointreau in a large pitcher. Gently pour in champagne. Stir to combine. Serve immediately. *Serves 6 – 8.*

ENERGY MATTERS

For those contemplating a new artificial Christmas tree, consider a fibre optic tree. These trees use a single low wattage lamp ranging from 5 to 50 watts depending on the size. Light is transmitted from the single lamp through hundreds of very small fibres.

For more energy saving ideas, visit www.atcoenergysense.com.

BLUEBERRY TEA

The flavour of this hot cocktail is reminiscent of blueberries.

1 cup (250 mL) freshly steeped hot strong Earl Grey tea
½ oz (15 mL) amaretto
½ oz (15 mL) Grand Marnier or other orange liqueur

Pour tea into a brandy snifter or a mug. Stir in amaretto and Grand Marnier. Serve immediately. *Serves 1.*

 Cook's Note: *ATCO Blue Flame Kitchen used Disaronno Originale Liqueur for the amaretto in this recipe.*

CHAI TEA

2 cups (500 mL) water
4 English breakfast tea bags
2 cups (500 mL) milk
2 tbsp (25 mL) honey
½ tsp (2 mL) cinnamon
½ tsp (2 mL) ground ginger
¼ tsp (1 mL) nutmeg

Bring water to a boil in a small saucepan. Add tea bags. Reduce heat and simmer, uncovered, for 2 minutes. Remove and discard tea bags. Stir in milk, honey, cinnamon, ginger and nutmeg. Bring to a boil over medium heat. Remove from heat.

Transfer mixture to a blender. Blend until frothy. Pour into mugs, spooning some foam onto each serving. It may be necessary to blend some of mixture a second time to create enough foam to top each serving. *Serves 4.*

 Cook's Note: *Mixture may also be foamed using a cappuccino machine or a milk frother.*

Blueberry Tea

SLOW COOKER WINTER COCKTAIL

1 bottle (1.89 L) cranberry raspberry cocktail
3 cups (750 mL) orange juice
½ cup (125 mL) brandy, optional
⅓ cup (75 mL) fresh lemon juice
¼ cup (50 mL) sugar
12 whole cloves
2 cinnamon sticks, broken

Combine cranberry raspberry cocktail, orange juice, brandy, lemon juice and sugar in a 5 quart (5 L) slow cooker. Place cloves and cinnamon sticks in a large tea ball or cheesecloth bag; add to slow cooker.

Cover and cook on high heat setting for 2½ – 3 hours. Remove tea ball before serving; discard contents. *Serves 8 – 10.*

MODERN MOCK CHAMPAGNE PUNCH

2 bottles (750 mL each) de-alcoholized sparkling wine, chilled
1 bottle (1.89 L) white cranberry cocktail, chilled
¾ cup (175 mL) thawed frozen lemonade concentrate
2 bottles (2 L each) ginger ale, chilled

Combine wine, white cranberry cocktail and lemonade concentrate in a large punch bowl. Stir in ginger ale. Serve immediately. *Makes about 30 cups (7.5 L).*

 Cook's Note: *ATCO Blue Flame Kitchen used Loxton Sparkling Brut for the de-alcoholized sparkling wine in this recipe.*

BAKING AND DESSERTS

Cashew Brown-Eyed Susans (page 105), Pineapple and Macadamia Nut Macaroons (page 123), Almond Toffee Squares (page 111)

CHIA SEEDS

Chia is a plant whose seeds contain omega-3 fatty acids, soluble fibre and various vitamins and minerals. Chia seeds are sold in natural food stores and specialty food stores.

PORRIDGE BREAD

½ cup (125 mL) cracked wheat, rye and flax cereal
½ cup (125 mL) boiling water
2 tbsp (25 mL) fancy molasses
¾ cup (175 mL) warm water (100°F/38°C)
1 tsp (5 mL) sugar
1 pkg (8 g) active dry yeast
1 cup (250 mL) flour
1 cup (250 mL) whole wheat flour
½ cup (125 mL) roasted pepitas (shelled pumpkin seeds)
   or sunflower seeds
1 tbsp (15 mL) chia seeds or poppy seeds
1 tbsp (15 mL) ground flaxseed
1 tbsp (15 mL) millet
1 tbsp (15 mL) sesame seeds
1 tsp (5 mL) salt
2 tbsp (25 mL) oil
Whole wheat flour, optional
Oil

Combine cereal and boiling water in a bowl. Let stand for 15 minutes. Stir in molasses; set aside.

Combine warm water and sugar, stirring to dissolve. Sprinkle yeast on top. Let stand until foamy, about 5 minutes.

Combine next 8 ingredients (flour through salt) in a stand mixer fitted with a dough hook. Add cereal mixture, yeast mixture and 2 tbsp (25 mL) oil. Using low speed, mix until combined and dough comes together and forms a ball, about 5 minutes. Dough will be soft. If dough is too sticky, gradually mix in additional whole wheat flour, 1 tbsp (15 mL) at a time, until dough comes together and forms a ball.

Turn dough out onto a floured surface. Using greased hands, shape dough into a loaf. Transfer loaf to a greased 8½x4½ inch (21x11 cm) loaf pan. Brush top of loaf with additional oil. Cover loosely with plastic wrap. Let loaf rise in a warm draft-free place until doubled in volume, about 50 – 60 minutes. Meanwhile, preheat oven to 350°F (180°C).

Bake for 35 – 40 minutes or until loaf is golden brown and sounds hollow when tapped. Invert loaf onto a rack and cool completely. May be frozen. *Makes 1.*

 Cook's Note: *ATCO Blue Flame Kitchen used The Original Red River Cereal for the cracked wheat, rye and flax cereal in this recipe.*

CASHEW BROWN-EYED SUSANS

1¾ cups (425 mL) flour
½ cup (125 mL) icing sugar
½ tsp (2 mL) baking powder
1 cup (250 mL) salted cashews
1 cup (250 mL) butter, softened
1 tsp (5 mL) vanilla
Milk chocolate pieces

Preheat oven to 350°F (180°C). Combine flour, icing sugar and baking powder in a bowl; set aside.

Place cashews in a food processor; process until finely chopped. Add butter and vanilla; process until smooth. Add flour mixture and process until dough comes together. Shape dough into 1¼ inch (3 cm) balls. Place balls 2 inches (5 cm) apart on parchment paper-lined cookie sheets. Gently press a chocolate piece into centre of each unbaked cookie, flattening cookie slightly.

Bake for 12 – 14 minutes or until cookies are light golden around edges. Let cookies stand for 5 minutes on cookie sheets. Remove from cookie sheets and cool cookies completely on racks. Store, layered with wax paper, in a cool dry place for up to 4 days. *Makes about 3½ dozen.*

 Cook's Note: *ATCO Blue Flame Kitchen used Cadbury Dairy Milk Buttons for the milk chocolate pieces. This recipe was also tested with unwrapped Hershey's Milk Chocolate Kisses.*

DID YOU KNOW?

Baking powder must be fresh to ensure success with baked goods. To check for freshness, combine 1 tsp (5 mL) baking powder and ⅓ cup (75 mL) hot water. This mixture should produce enthusiastic bubbling.

*Use a good-quality, full-fat ice cream
in recipes that require the ice cream to
be softened. Do not use light ice cream
as it may develop ice crystals after being
softened and then refrozen.*

GINGER TOFFEE BOMBE

1⅓ cups (325 mL) gingersnap crumbs
¼ cup (50 mL) butter, melted
4 cups (1 L) vanilla ice cream, softened
4 butter toffee chocolate bars (39 g each), crushed
1 tsp (5 mL) vanilla
½ tsp (2 mL) ground ginger
Praline Sauce (recipe follows)

Line a 6 cup (1.5 L) bowl with plastic wrap. Combine crumbs and melted
butter until blended. Press crumb mixture onto bottom and up sides of
prepared bowl. Cover and freeze while preparing filling.

To prepare filling, combine ice cream, crushed chocolate bars, vanilla and
ginger. Remove crumb-lined bowl from freezer. Spoon ice cream mixture
into crumb-lined bowl. Cover and freeze for at least 8 hours or up to 1 week.

To serve, remove bombe from freezer and let stand at room temperature for
5 minutes. Invert bombe onto a serving plate. Remove plastic wrap. Cut
into wedges and serve with warm Praline Sauce. *Serves 10.*

 Cook's Note: *ATCO Blue Flame Kitchen used Skor chocolate bars in
this recipe.*

PRALINE SAUCE

½ cup (125 mL) packed brown sugar
½ cup (125 mL) whipping cream
¼ cup (50 mL) butter
¼ cup (50 mL) chopped toasted almonds
1 tsp (5 mL) vanilla

Combine brown sugar, cream and butter in a small saucepan. Bring to a boil
over medium heat, stirring frequently. Boil, stirring constantly, for 2 minutes.
Remove from heat. Stir in almonds and vanilla. May be prepared in advance
and refrigerated for up to 24 hours. Reheat over low heat. *Makes 1 cup (250 mL).*

Lemon Loaf

1½ cups (375 mL) flour
1½ tsp (7 mL) baking powder
¼ tsp (1 mL) salt
⅓ cup (75 mL) butter, softened
1 cup (250 mL) sugar
½ cup (125 mL) milk
2 eggs
1½ tsp (7 mL) grated lemon peel
⅓ cup (75 mL) sugar
3 tbsp (40 mL) fresh lemon juice

Preheat oven to 350°F (180°C). Combine flour, baking powder and salt in a bowl; set aside.

Beat together butter and 1 cup (250 mL) sugar until fluffy. Whisk together milk, eggs and lemon peel. Add milk mixture to butter mixture and stir until blended. Add mixture to flour mixture and stir just until combined. Spoon batter into a greased 8½x4½ inch (21x11 cm) loaf pan.

Bake for 1 hour or until a cake tester inserted in centre comes out clean. Cool in pan on a rack for 5 minutes. Meanwhile, to prepare glaze, stir together ⅓ cup (75 mL) sugar and lemon juice until combined.

Drizzle glaze over top of loaf, allowing glaze to run down sides of loaf. Cool in pan on rack for 10 minutes. Invert loaf onto rack and cool completely. May be frozen. *Makes 1.*

Did you know?

For best results when baking, allow eggs to stand at room temperature for 30 minutes before using in a recipe.

CHERRY BLOSSOM COOKIES

1¾ cups (425 mL) flour
1 tsp (5 mL) baking powder
½ cup (125 mL) butter, softened
1 cup (250 mL) packed brown sugar
1 cup (250 mL) semi-sweet chocolate chips, melted and cooled
1 egg
1 tsp (5 mL) almond extract
65 – 70 maraschino cherries, drained and patted dry
Chocolate Cherry Glaze (recipe on page 109)
Slivered maraschino cherries, optional

Preheat oven to 350°F (180°C). Combine flour and baking powder in a bowl; set aside.

Using medium speed of an electric mixer, beat together butter and brown sugar until fluffy. Beat in cooled melted chocolate chips, egg and almond extract until blended. Beat in flour mixture just until combined. Shape dough into 1 inch (2.5 cm) balls. Flatten each ball and place a cherry in centre. Wrap dough around cherry and reshape into a ball. Place balls 2 inches (5 cm) apart on parchment paper-lined cookie sheets.

Bake for 10 – 12 minutes or until tops of cookies are cracked. Let cookies stand for 5 minutes on cookie sheets. Remove from cookie sheets and cool cookies completely on racks.

Spread with Chocolate Cherry Glaze and top each cookie with a slivered cherry piece. Let stand until glaze is set. Store, layered with wax paper, in an airtight container in a cool dry place for up to 2 days. May be frozen.
Makes about 5½ dozen.

 Cook's Note: *ATCO Blue Flame Kitchen used one 375 mL jar and some of a second 375 mL jar of Daltons Maraschino Cherries in this recipe.*

Chocolate Cherry Glaze

1 cup (250 mL) semi-sweet chocolate chips
2 tbsp (25 mL) maraschino cherry syrup
1 tbsp (15 mL) butter

Combine chocolate chips, syrup and butter in a small nonreactive saucepan. Cook over low heat, stirring, until chocolate is melted and mixture is smooth.

Foolproof Pastry

This easy-to-roll pastry is great for a novice cook.

3 cups (750 mL) flour
½ tsp (2 mL) salt
1 cup (250 mL) shortening, chilled and cubed
6 tbsp (90 mL) ice water
1 tsp (5 mL) pure white vinegar
1 egg, lightly beaten
Ice water, optional

Combine flour and salt in a bowl. Cut in shortening with a pastry blender until mixture resembles coarse meal. Whisk together 6 tbsp (90 mL) ice water, vinegar and beaten egg. Gradually add ice water mixture to flour mixture, mixing lightly with a fork just until dough starts to hold together. If dough is too dry, gradually mix in additional ice water, 1 tsp (5 mL) at a time, just until dough comes together. Gather dough into a ball; divide in half. Flatten each half into a disc shape. Wrap each disc with plastic wrap and refrigerate for 2 hours before rolling out.
Makes 1 double or 2 single 9 inch (23 cm) crust(s).

 Cook's Note: *If desired, this dough may be used to make tart shells. On a lightly floured surface, roll out dough ⅛ inch (3 mm) thick. Using a floured 4 inch (10 cm) cookie cutter, cut dough into rounds. Transfer each round to a muffin cup or tart cup; press into cup to form a tart shell. Makes about 24 tart shells (4 inch/10 cm each).*

Did You Know?

Always roll pastry dough from the centre out, not back and forth. Turn dough occasionally as you roll to keep an even thickness and round shape. It is important to roll out as lightly and as little as possible so as not to overwork the dough.

JEWELLED LIGHT FRUITCAKE

This light-coloured fruitcake is attractive when sliced due to its jewel-toned fruit. It makes a wonderful addition to a tray of baking.

2 cups (500 mL) chopped glacé mixed peel (candied mixed peel)
2 cups (500 mL) coarsely chopped dried mango
1½ cups (375 mL) golden raisins
1½ cups (375 mL) blanched whole almonds
1 cup (250 mL) coarsely chopped glacé pineapple (candied pineapple)
1 cup (250 mL) whole green glacé cherries (green candied cherries)
1 cup (250 mL) whole red glacé cherries (red candied cherries)
1 cup (250 mL) flour
1 cup (250 mL) butter, softened
1¼ cups (300 mL) sugar
5 eggs
1 can (14 oz/398 mL) crushed pineapple, drained and squeezed dry
1 tbsp (15 mL) grated lemon peel
1 tsp (5 mL) vanilla
½ tsp (2 mL) almond extract
2 cups (500 mL) flour
1 tsp (5 mL) salt

Preheat oven to 275°F (140°C). Line bottom and sides of two greased 9x5 inch (23x13 cm) loaf pans with parchment paper.

Combine first 7 ingredients (mixed peel through cherries) in a large bowl. Add 1 cup (250 mL) flour and toss to coat; set aside.

Using medium speed of an electric mixer, beat together butter and sugar until fluffy. Beat in eggs, one at a time, beating well after each addition. Beat in crushed pineapple, lemon peel, vanilla and almond extract until blended. Combine 2 cups (500 mL) flour and salt in a bowl. Using low speed of an electric mixer, beat flour mixture into butter mixture until smooth. Add mixture to fruit mixture and stir to combine. Spoon batter into prepared pans and spread evenly.

Bake for 2 – 2¼ hours or until cakes are light golden and a cake tester inserted in centres comes out clean. Cake tester may be sticky from fruit, but should not be wet from batter. Cool cakes completely in pans on racks. Invert cakes onto racks and remove parchment paper. Wrap cakes with plastic wrap. Transfer wrapped cakes to zip-lock plastic bags.

Store cakes in a cool dry place for 3 – 4 weeks. Allowing cakes to season improves the flavour and makes them easier to slice. Check cakes for mould at least once a week. If mould should occur, discard cakes. Once seasoned, store cakes in the refrigerator or freezer. *Makes 2.*

ALMOND TOFFEE SQUARES

26 graham wafers
1 cup (250 mL) butter
1 cup (250 mL) packed golden brown sugar
2 cups (500 mL) milk chocolate chips
1 cup (250 mL) slivered almonds, toasted and chopped

Line a 10x15 inch (25x38 cm) rimmed baking sheet with nonstick foil. Place graham wafers in a single layer in prepared pan, cutting graham wafers as needed to fill pan. Graham wafers should fit tightly; set aside.

Place butter and brown sugar in a small heavy saucepan. Bring to a boil over medium heat, stirring frequently. Reduce heat and cook, stirring constantly, for 5 minutes. Pour butter mixture over graham wafers and spread evenly. Let stand for 3 minutes.

Sprinkle chocolate chips in a single layer on top of butter mixture. Let stand for 4 minutes or until chocolate chips are almost melted. Spread melted chocolate chips evenly over butter mixture. Sprinkle with almonds. Refrigerate, uncovered, until firm.

Remove pan from refrigerator. Let stand for 20 – 30 minutes. Using foil as an aid, lift square from pan and cut into squares. Remove squares from foil. Store, layered with wax paper, in an airtight container in a cool dry place for up to 1 week. May be frozen. *Makes 60.*

SAFETY MATTERS

When you install a new carbon monoxide detector, write the expiry date on top of the detector.

For more safety tips, visit www.atcogas.com.

STICKY TOFFEE PUDDINGS

¾ cup (175 mL) water
½ cup (125 mL) diced pitted dates
½ cup (125 mL) dried cranberries
1 tsp (5 mL) baking soda
1 cup (250 mL) flour
1 tsp (5 mL) baking powder
½ tsp (2 mL) salt
⅓ cup (75 mL) butter, softened
¾ cup (175 mL) packed dark brown sugar
2 eggs
1 tsp (5 mL) vanilla
1 cup (250 mL) packed dark brown sugar
½ cup (125 mL) butter
½ cup (125 mL) whipping cream
1 tsp (5 mL) vanilla
¼ tsp (1 mL) salt
Whipped cream

Preheat oven to 350°F (180°C). Combine water and dates in a small nonreactive saucepan. Bring to a boil over medium heat. Reduce heat and simmer, uncovered, stirring occasionally, for 5 minutes or until dates are softened. Remove from heat. Stir in cranberries and baking soda; cool to room temperature.

Combine flour, baking powder and ½ tsp (2 mL) salt in a bowl; set aside. Using medium speed of an electric mixer, beat together ⅓ cup (75 mL) butter and ¾ cup (175 mL) brown sugar until fluffy. Beat in eggs, one at a time, beating well after each addition. Beat in 1 tsp (5 mL) vanilla. Add flour mixture to butter mixture and beat just until blended, about 1 minute. Stir in date mixture. Spoon batter into greased muffin cups, filling cups three-quarters full.

Bake for 12 – 15 minutes or until a cake tester inserted in centres comes out clean. Meanwhile, to prepare sauce, combine 1 cup (250 mL) brown sugar, ½ cup (125 mL) butter and cream in a small saucepan. Bring to a boil over medium heat, stirring frequently. Reduce heat and cook, stirring frequently, until slightly thickened, about 7 – 8 minutes. Remove from heat. Stir in 1 tsp (5 mL) vanilla and ¼ tsp (1 mL) salt; set aside.

Cool puddings in pan for 5 minutes. Remove from pan and place, top side down, on individual dessert plates. Serve warm with sauce and whipped cream. *Makes 12.*

Sticky Toffee Puddings

DID YOU KNOW?

Whipping cream is measured before whipping. It may or may not get whipped in the recipe. Whipped cream is measured after whipping.

COFFEE BAVARIANS

¼ cup (50 mL) cold water
1 envelope unflavoured gelatin
2 cups (500 mL) light cream (10%)
½ cup (125 mL) sugar
2 tbsp (25 mL) unsweetened cocoa powder
½ tsp (2 mL) vanilla
3 tbsp (40 mL) instant coffee granules
½ cup (125 mL) whipping cream
1 tbsp (15 mL) icing sugar
½ tsp (2 mL) cinnamon

Place cold water in a small saucepan. Sprinkle gelatin over water and let stand for 5 minutes or until softened. Meanwhile, place light cream, sugar, cocoa and vanilla in a blender. Blend until combined; set aside.

Cook gelatin mixture over low heat, stirring until gelatin is dissolved. Add coffee granules, stirring until dissolved. Remove from heat and stir in ¼ cup (50 mL) of cream mixture.

With blender running, pour coffee mixture through opening in lid in a thin steady stream, blending until well combined, about 30 seconds. Pour mixture into small cappuccino cups. Cover and refrigerate for at least 4 hours or up to 2 days.

Using medium speed of an electric mixer, beat together whipping cream, icing sugar and cinnamon until stiff. Top each serving with a dollop of whipped cream mixture. *Serves 6 – 8.*

OLD-FASHIONED BUTTER TARTS

¾ cup (175 mL) sultana raisins
Boiling water
⅓ cup (75 mL) butter
¾ cup (175 mL) golden corn syrup
¾ cup (175 mL) packed golden brown sugar
2 tbsp (25 mL) light cream (10%)
1½ tsp (7 mL) vanilla
1 tsp (5 mL) fresh lemon juice
¼ tsp (1 mL) salt
1 egg, lightly beaten
24 frozen unbaked tart shells (3 inch/7.5 cm)

Place raisins in a bowl; pour enough boiling water over raisins to cover. Let stand for 5 minutes; drain. Pat raisins dry with paper towels; set aside.

Preheat oven to 350°F (180°C). Melt butter in a medium saucepan over medium heat. Remove from heat and whisk in next 7 ingredients (corn syrup through beaten egg).

Return saucepan to medium heat. Bring butter mixture to a boil. Boil, uncovered, stirring occasionally, for 3 minutes. Remove from heat and cool for 5 minutes. Meanwhile, spoon raisins into tart shells, dividing equally.

Transfer tart shells to parchment paper-lined rimmed baking sheets. Spoon butter mixture on top of raisins in tart shells, filling tart shells no more than half full.

Bake for 20 – 25 minutes or until filling is bubbly and pastry is golden around edges. Cool tarts completely in pans on racks. Store, layered with wax paper, in an airtight container in a cool dry place for up to 1 week. May be frozen. *Makes 24.*

SAFETY MATTERS

Open the damper in your fireplace and crack open a window before lighting your wood-burning fireplace. This allows the smoke and gases to exit, keeping you and your family safe from carbon monoxide poisoning.

For more safety tips, visit www.atcogas.com.

LEMON PEEL

Grated lemon peel is also known as grated lemon rind or zest. These terms refer to the outermost coloured portion of the skin, but not the bitter white part, or pith, underneath.

CHOCOLATE WHOOPIE PIES

A whoopie pie is a cake-like sandwich cookie. The whoopie pies in this recipe have a lemon ginger filling.

1 cup (250 mL) milk
1 tbsp (15 mL) pure white vinegar
2 cups (500 mL) flour
½ cup (125 mL) unsweetened cocoa powder, sifted
2 tsp (10 mL) ground ginger
1 tsp (5 mL) baking soda
1 tsp (5 mL) salt
½ cup (125 mL) butter, softened
1 cup (250 mL) packed dark brown sugar
1 egg
1 tbsp (15 mL) grated lemon peel
1 tsp (5 mL) vanilla
8 oz (250 g) cream cheese, softened
¼ cup (50 mL) butter, softened
1 tbsp (15 mL) fresh lemon juice
1 cup (250 mL) icing sugar
1 tsp (5 mL) grated lemon peel
1 tsp (5 mL) ground ginger

Preheat oven to 350°F (180°C). Combine milk and vinegar; set aside. Combine flour, cocoa, 2 tsp (10 mL) ginger, baking soda and salt in a bowl; set aside.

Using medium speed of an electric mixer, beat together ½ cup (125 mL) butter and brown sugar until fluffy. Beat in egg, 1 tbsp (15 mL) lemon peel and vanilla until blended. Mixing by hand with a wooden spoon or rubber spatula and beginning and ending with flour mixture, add flour mixture alternately with milk mixture to butter mixture, stirring just until blended. Spoon 32 equal mounds of batter, each measuring about 1 tbsp (15 mL), 2 inches (5 cm) apart onto parchment paper-lined cookie sheets.

Bake for 10 – 12 minutes or until cookies are puffed and tops spring back when lightly touched. Let cookies stand for 3 minutes on cookie sheets. Remove from cookie sheets and cool cookies completely on racks. Meanwhile, to prepare filling, use medium speed of an electric mixer and beat together cream cheese, ¼ cup (50 mL) butter and lemon juice until smooth. Gradually beat in icing sugar, 1 tsp (5 mL) lemon peel and 1 tsp (5 mL) ginger until fluffy.

Spoon about 1 tbsp (15 mL) filling onto flat bottom of 16 cookies. Place a cookie, flat side down, on top of each filling mound, making sandwiches. Refrigerate until serving. May be frozen for up to 1 month. Thaw in refrigerator. *Makes 16.*

GREEN TEA SHORTBREAD

3 – 4 green tea bags
2 cups (500 mL) flour
¼ tsp (1 mL) salt
1 cup (250 mL) butter, softened
½ cup (125 mL) icing sugar
½ tsp (2 mL) vanilla

Preheat oven to 325°F (160°C). Grind contents of tea bags in a coffee grinder; discard bags. There should be about 2 tbsp (25 mL) ground tea. Combine ground tea, flour and salt in a bowl; set aside.

Using medium speed of an electric mixer, beat butter until creamy. Add icing sugar and beat until fluffy. Beat in vanilla. Using low speed, beat in flour mixture just until combined. Gather dough into a ball; flatten into a disc shape. On a lightly floured surface, roll out dough ¼ inch (6 mm) thick. Using a small decorative cookie cutter, cut dough into shapes. Place 1 inch (2.5 cm) apart on parchment paper-lined cookie sheets.

Bake for 15 – 17 minutes or just until cookies are firm and lightly browned on bottoms. Do not overbake. Let cookies stand for 1 minute on cookie sheets. Remove from cookie sheets and cool cookies completely on racks. Store in an airtight container in a cool dry place for up to 1 week. May be frozen. *Makes 3½ – 4 dozen.*

DID YOU KNOW?

The amount of flour required for shortbread may vary with the different brands of flour. Work the last ¼ – ⅓ cup (50 – 75 mL) flour into the mixture until the desired consistency is obtained.

SPICY GINGERBREAD MEN

2 cups (500 mL) flour
1½ tsp (7 mL) cinnamon
1 tsp (5 mL) baking powder
1 tsp (5 mL) ground cloves
1 tsp (5 mL) ground ginger
½ tsp (2 mL) nutmeg
½ tsp (2 mL) baking soda
½ tsp (2 mL) salt
½ cup (125 mL) shortening
½ cup (125 mL) fancy molasses
½ cup (125 mL) sugar
1 egg yolk
Royal Frosting (recipe on page 120)
Assorted candy

Combine first 8 ingredients (flour through salt) in a bowl; set aside. Using medium speed of an electric mixer, beat together shortening, molasses and sugar until fluffy. Add egg yolk and continue beating until blended. Using low speed, gradually beat in flour mixture just until combined. Gather dough into a ball; flatten into a disc shape. Wrap disc with plastic wrap and refrigerate for 1 hour before rolling out.

Preheat oven to 350°F (180°C). Remove dough from refrigerator. On a lightly floured surface, roll out dough ¼ inch (6 mm) thick. Using a 3½ inch (9 cm) tall gingerbread man cookie cutter, cut dough into shapes. Using a floured spatula, place 2 inches (5 cm) apart on ungreased cookie sheets.

Bake for 10 minutes or until lightly browned. Let cookies stand for 5 minutes on cookie sheets. Remove from cookie sheets and cool cookies completely on racks. Decorate cookies using Royal Frosting and candy.
Makes about 2 dozen.

When doubled, this recipe makes enough dough to build a gingerbread house. Divide dough in half, flatten into rectangles, wrap and refrigerate for 1 hour before rolling out. Roll out dough ¼ inch (6 mm) thick, cut into house pieces and bake until lightly browned. Leftover dough may be re-rolled and cut into shapes for cookies.

For full gingerbread house instructions and pattern dimension diagrams, visit www.atcoblueflamekitchen.com or call the ATCO Blue Flame Kitchen Answer Line at 1.877.420.9090.

Spicy Gingerbread House (www.atcoblueflamekitchen.com)

MAKING COOKIE HOUSES

Cookie houses can be made with graham wafers. Attach graham wafers using royal frosting and decorate with assorted candy. Each house requires seven graham wafers. Use one graham wafer for the base, four for the walls and two for the roof.

ROYAL FROSTING

6 tbsp (90 mL) pasteurized liquid egg whites
1½ tsp (7 mL) cream of tartar
3½ cups (875 mL) icing sugar, sifted

Using high speed of an electric mixer, beat liquid egg whites until foamy. Add cream of tartar and continue beating until very stiff. Gradually beat in icing sugar until stiff peaks form. Spoon frosting into a pastry bag fitted with a large plain tip. Frosting becomes hard upon standing uncovered. May be refrigerated in an airtight container for up to 24 hours.
Makes about 2 cups (500 mL).

 Cook's Note: *In recipes where the egg remains uncooked or lightly cooked, it is recommended that pasteurized egg products be used. Pasteurized egg products, such as liquid egg whites and liquid whole egg, are available in the refrigerator or freezer section of most grocery stores. ATCO Blue Flame Kitchen used Burnbrae Farms Naturegg Simply Egg Whites in this recipe.*

CHOCOLATE BAKLAVA

2½ cups (625 mL) shelled pistachios, toasted and cooled
2 tbsp (25 mL) sugar
½ tsp (2 mL) cinnamon
6 squares bittersweet or dark chocolate, finely chopped
½ cup (125 mL) butter, melted, divided
12 sheets phyllo pastry, halved crosswise
1½ cups (375 mL) orange juice
1½ cups (375 mL) sugar
¾ cup (175 mL) honey
2 tbsp (25 mL) fresh lemon juice
2 strips lemon peel (3x½ inch/7.5x1.25 cm)

To prepare filling, place pistachios, 2 tbsp (25 mL) sugar and cinnamon in a food processor; process, using an on/off motion, until pistachios are finely chopped. Transfer pistachio mixture to a bowl. Add chocolate and stir to combine; set aside. There should be about 4 cups (1 L) filling.

Preheat oven to 350°F (180°C). Line a 9x13 inch (23x33 cm) baking pan with parchment paper, leaving a 2 inch (5 cm) overhang; lightly brush parchment paper with some of the melted butter.

Brush top of one piece of phyllo with some of the melted butter. Place in prepared pan. Lay five additional pieces of phyllo on top, brushing each with melted butter. Sprinkle with 1 cup (250 mL) filling.

Brush top of one piece of phyllo with melted butter. Place on top of filling. Lay three additional pieces of phyllo on top, brushing each with melted butter. Sprinkle with 1 cup (250 mL) filling. Repeat procedure two times, each time using four pieces of phyllo, melted butter and 1 cup (250 mL) filling.

Brush top of one piece of phyllo with melted butter. Place on top of filling. Lay remaining five pieces of phyllo on top, brushing each with remaining melted butter. Carefully cut through top 6 layers of phyllo in a criss-cross fashion to make diamonds. Cover phyllo with a piece of parchment paper. Place an empty 9x13 inch (23x33 cm) baking pan of the same size, bottom side down, on top of parchment paper. Fill empty pan with pie weights, dried beans or raw rice to weigh layers down.

Place pans in oven and bake for 40 – 45 minutes or until golden brown. Meanwhile, to prepare syrup, combine orange juice, 1½ cups (375 mL) sugar, honey, lemon juice and lemon peel in a medium nonreactive saucepan. Bring to a boil over medium heat. Reduce heat and simmer, stirring, for 1 minute. Remove and discard lemon peel. Syrup will be thin; keep warm.

Remove pans from oven. Remove pan with pie weights from bottom pan. Remove top piece of parchment paper from phyllo. Pour hot syrup evenly over phyllo. Cool baklava completely in pan on a rack. Using parchment paper as an aid, lift baklava from pan and cut completely into diamonds. Store, layered with wax paper, in an airtight container in a cool dry place for up to 3 days. May be frozen.
Makes about 40 depending on cut size of diamonds.

PHYLLO

Phyllo is paper-thin layers of pastry dough used in Greek and Middle Eastern sweet or savoury preparations. It is available frozen in most grocery stores. Thaw phyllo in its original wrapping in the refrigerator.

CINNAMON WALNUT BARS

2 cups (500 mL) flour
¼ cup (50 mL) sugar
½ tsp (2 mL) cinnamon
¾ cup (175 mL) butter, chilled and cubed
⅔ cup (150 mL) white corn syrup
2 tbsp (25 mL) honey
2 tbsp (25 mL) sugar
2 tbsp (25 mL) fresh lemon juice
1 tbsp (15 mL) butter, melted
2 eggs, lightly beaten
2 tsp (10 mL) cinnamon
½ tsp (2 mL) grated lemon peel
½ tsp (2 mL) vanilla
¼ tsp (1 mL) salt
2 cups (500 mL) chopped walnuts
Cinnamon Glaze (recipe on page 123)

Preheat oven to 350°F (180°C). To prepare crust, place flour, ¼ cup (50 mL) sugar and ½ tsp (2 mL) cinnamon in a food processor; process to combine. Add ¾ cup (175 mL) butter and process, using an on/off motion, until mixture is crumbly. Press mixture into a greased 9x13 inch (23x33 cm) baking pan.

Bake for 20 minutes or until light golden. Meanwhile, whisk together next 10 ingredients (corn syrup through salt). Stir in walnuts. Remove pan from oven. Immediately spread walnut mixture over hot crust.

Continue baking for 20 – 25 minutes or until set. Cool in pan on a rack for 10 minutes. Run a knife around sides of pan to loosen; cool completely in pan on rack. Drizzle with Cinnamon Glaze. Let stand until glaze is set. Cut into bars. May be frozen. *Makes 48.*

Cinnamon Glaze

1 cup (250 mL) icing sugar
1 tbsp (15 mL) honey
½ tsp (2 mL) fresh lemon juice
½ tsp (2 mL) cinnamon
Hot water

Combine icing sugar, honey, lemon juice and cinnamon. Add 1 tbsp (15 mL) hot water, stirring until mixture is smooth. If mixture is too thick, stir in additional hot water, 1 tsp (5 mL) at a time, until mixture is of drizzling consistency.

Pineapple and Macadamia Nut Macaroons

4 egg whites
¼ tsp (1 mL) salt
⅔ cup (150 mL) sugar
¼ cup (50 mL) flour
1 tbsp (15 mL) grated orange peel
1 tsp (5 mL) vanilla
3 cups (750 mL) sweetened shredded coconut
1 cup (250 mL) coarsely chopped glacé pineapple (candied pineapple)
¾ cup (175 mL) coarsely chopped macadamia nuts

Preheat oven to 325°F (160°C). Using medium speed of an electric mixer, beat egg whites and salt until stiff peaks form. Gradually beat in sugar, flour, orange peel and vanilla until blended. Fold in coconut, pineapple and macadamia nuts. Drop rounded 1 tbsp (15 mL) measures of mixture 1 inch (2.5 cm) apart onto parchment paper-lined cookie sheets. Flatten tops slightly.

Bake for 15 – 20 minutes or until light golden. Let macaroons stand for 5 minutes on cookie sheets. Remove from cookie sheets and cool macaroons on racks. Store, layered with wax paper, in an airtight container for up to 4 days. May be frozen. *Makes about 5 dozen.*

Did You Know?

For a festive touch, place a doily or Christmas stencil on top of an unfrosted cake. Sift icing sugar over doily. Remove doily from cake and serve.

There is a difference between pure pumpkin and pumpkin pie filling. Both products are sold canned and usually found side by side in the baking aisle of grocery stores. Pure pumpkin is pumpkin with no added ingredients. Pumpkin pie filling has other ingredients such as sugar, oil, salt and spices added to it. Check the labels carefully as these products are not interchangeable.

STEAMED PUMPKIN PUDDING WITH GINGER SABAYON

Serve this cake-like pudding with our Ginger Sabayon or your favourite sauce.

2 cups (500 mL) flour
½ cup (125 mL) finely chopped pecans
1½ tsp (7 mL) baking soda
1½ tsp (7 mL) cinnamon
1 tsp (5 mL) ground ginger
1 tsp (5 mL) salt
¾ tsp (3 mL) nutmeg
¼ tsp (1 mL) ground cloves
3 eggs
1 cup (250 mL) packed golden brown sugar
1½ cups (375 mL) canned pure pumpkin
¼ cup (50 mL) fancy molasses
¼ cup (50 mL) butter, melted
Ginger Sabayon (recipe on page 125)

Combine first 8 ingredients (flour through cloves) in a bowl; set aside. Using medium speed of an electric mixer, beat together eggs and brown sugar until thick and pale in colour, about 3 minutes. Beat in pumpkin and molasses until blended. Gradually beat in flour mixture just until blended. Stir in melted butter just until combined. Spoon batter into a greased 2 quart (2 L) pudding mould.

Place greased lid on mould or cover tightly with greased foil. Secure foil by tying string around sides of mould. Place mould on a rack in a large pot. Add enough boiling water to come halfway up sides of mould. Cover pot and bring to a boil. Reduce heat and simmer, covered, adding additional boiling water as required, for 2 hours or until pudding tests done.

Remove mould from pot and cool pudding in mould on a rack for 15 minutes. Invert pudding onto a plate. Serve warm with Ginger Sabayon. Alternatively, invert pudding onto rack and cool completely. Freeze for up to 1 month. If freezing, thaw pudding in refrigerator before reheating. To reheat, place pudding in same greased pudding mould. Follow recipe directions for steaming pudding and simmer, covered, for 30 – 40 minutes or until heated through. *Serves 10 – 12.*

GINGER SABAYON

Sabayon is a rich, light and frothy custard that can be used as a dessert sauce. It is great served over cake or fresh fruit.

> **4 egg yolks**
> **1 egg**
> **½ cup (125 mL) orange juice**
> **½ cup (125 mL) sugar**
> **2 tbsp (25 mL) Grand Marnier or other orange liqueur**
> **1 tbsp (15 mL) finely chopped drained preserved ginger**
> **1 tbsp (15 mL) syrup from preserved ginger**

Whisk together all ingredients in a medium stainless steel bowl until blended. Set bowl over a saucepan of simmering water. Do not allow water to touch bowl. Cook mixture, whisking constantly, until mixture is thickened, frothy and pale yellow in colour, about 10 minutes. Mixture should almost double in volume. Remove from heat and let stand for 1 minute. Serve immediately. Do not hold or reheat sabayon. *Makes about 2⅓ cups (575 mL).*

EASY DECORATING TIP

Place a tall pillar candle in a glass bowl and fill the bowl with a mixture of pine cones and unshelled nuts.

NUTMEG SCONES WITH GINGER BUTTER

2 cups (500 mL) flour
⅓ cup (75 mL) packed golden brown sugar
2 tsp (10 mL) baking powder
1¼ tsp (6 mL) nutmeg
½ tsp (2 mL) baking soda
½ tsp (2 mL) salt
½ cup (125 mL) butter, chilled and cubed
1 cup (250 mL) sour cream
2 tsp (10 mL) sugar
Ginger Butter (recipe follows)

Preheat oven to 425°F (220°C). Combine first 6 ingredients (flour through salt) in a bowl. Cut in butter with a pastry blender until mixture is crumbly. Add sour cream and stir just until combined. Dough will be soft.

Turn dough out onto a lightly floured surface. Knead dough gently 5 times. Roll out dough into a 4x10 inch (10x25 cm) rectangle. Using a knife, cut dough into 10 squares. Sprinkle tops with sugar. Place on an ungreased cookie sheet.

Bake for 15 – 20 minutes or until golden brown. Serve with Ginger Butter. *Makes 10.*

GINGER BUTTER

¾ cup (175 mL) butter, softened
3 tbsp (40 mL) finely chopped drained preserved ginger
2 tsp (10 mL) syrup from preserved ginger

Using medium speed of an electric mixer, beat together all ingredients until fluffy. Cover and refrigerate for up to 1 week. *Makes about 1 cup (250 mL).*

GIFTS FROM THE KITCHEN

Easy Marshmallow Fudge (page 128)

EASY MARSHMALLOW FUDGE

3 cups (750 mL) sugar
¾ cup (175 mL) butter
¾ cup (175 mL) canned evaporated milk
2½ cups (625 mL) miniature marshmallows
2 cups (500 mL) semi-sweet chocolate chips
1 tsp (5 mL) vanilla
1 cup (250 mL) coarsely chopped nuts

Line an 8 inch (20 cm) square baking pan with nonstick foil, leaving a 2 inch (5 cm) overhang.

Combine sugar, butter and evaporated milk in a medium saucepan over medium heat. Bring to a full rolling boil, stirring frequently. Cook, stirring, for 3 minutes. Remove from heat.

Add marshmallows, chocolate chips and vanilla, stirring until marshmallows and chocolate chips are melted. Stir in walnuts. Pour into prepared pan. Refrigerate, uncovered, until firm.

Using foil as an aid, lift fudge from pan and cut into squares. Remove squares from foil. Store in an airtight container in refrigerator for up to 1 week. May be frozen. *Makes 36.*

 Cook's Note: *One bag (350 g) semi-sweet chocolate chips contains 2 cups (500 mL).*

GRANDMA'S POPPYCOCK

24 cups (6 L) popped popcorn
1½ cups (375 mL) toasted pecans, coarsely chopped
1½ cups (375 mL) toasted whole natural almonds, coarsely chopped
1 cup (250 mL) butter
1½ cups (375 mL) sugar
1 cup (250 mL) white corn syrup
½ tsp (2 mL) baking soda
½ tsp (2 mL) cream of tartar
½ tsp (2 mL) salt
½ tsp (2 mL) vanilla

Grease two large rimmed baking sheets. Combine popcorn, pecans and almonds in a greased large bowl; set aside.

Melt butter in a medium saucepan over medium heat. Add sugar and corn syrup; cook, stirring, until mixture boils. Reduce heat and simmer gently, uncovered, without stirring, until soft-ball stage is reached (240°F/116°C on a candy thermometer). Remove from heat and immediately stir in baking soda, cream of tartar, salt and vanilla. Mixture will foam.

Pour sugar mixture over popcorn mixture and stir gently to coat. Spread popcorn mixture in a single layer in prepared pans. Cool completely in pans.

Break popcorn mixture into clusters. Store in an airtight container in a cool dry place for up to 4 days or freeze for up to 1 month.
Makes about 28 cups (7 L).

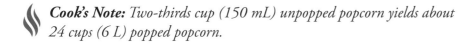 **Cook's Note:** *Two-thirds cup (150 mL) unpopped popcorn yields about 24 cups (6 L) popped popcorn.*

DID YOU KNOW?

Baking soda must be fresh to ensure success. To check for freshness, combine 1 tsp (5 mL) baking soda, ⅓ cup (75 mL) hot water and 1 tsp (5 mL) vinegar. This mixture should produce bubbling.

UNSWEETENED COCOA POWDER

Solid chocolate contains both chocolate liquor and cocoa butter. The chocolate liquor gives chocolate its characteristic taste and colour, while cocoa butter imparts a smooth creamy texture. The residue left after cocoa butter has been pressed from the chocolate liquor is dried and ground into unsweetened cocoa powder.

BALSAMIC CHOCOLATE TRUFFLES

2 cups (500 mL) finely chopped dark chocolate dipping wafers
1 cup (250 mL) finely chopped milk chocolate dipping wafers
¾ cup (175 mL) whipping cream
⅓ cup (75 mL) balsamic vinegar glaze
Unsweetened cocoa powder, sifted

Combine dipping wafers in a heatproof bowl; set aside. Heat cream in a small saucepan over medium heat until steaming and just beginning to simmer. Do not boil. Pour hot cream over dipping wafers and let stand for 2 minutes. Using a whisk, stir until chocolate is melted and mixture is smooth. Stir in balsamic vinegar glaze. Cover and refrigerate for up to 8 hours or until firm enough to handle.

Shape mixture into 1 inch (2.5 cm) balls. If mixture becomes too soft to handle, return mixture to refrigerator until firm. Roll balls in cocoa until coated. Store, layered with wax paper, in an airtight container in refrigerator for up to 1 week. May be frozen. *Makes about 5 dozen.*

 Cook's Note: *Balsamic vinegar glaze is a balsamic vinegar reduction that has the consistency of a thin syrup. It is usually available in grocery stores where vinegars are sold. It is also available in Italian grocery stores and specialty food stores.*

ROCKY ROAD BARK

4 cups (1 L) dark chocolate dipping wafers
2 cups (500 mL) chopped walnuts
2 cups (500 mL) miniature marshmallows

Line a 10x15 inch (25x38 cm) rimmed baking sheet with nonstick foil. Melt dipping wafers in a large heavy saucepan over low heat, stirring frequently until smooth. Remove from heat and cool for 5 minutes.

Gently stir walnuts and marshmallows into melted chocolate. Spread mixture evenly in prepared pan. Refrigerate for 1 hour or until firm.

Break bark into pieces. Store in an airtight container in a cool dry place for up to 1 week or freeze for up to 6 weeks. *Makes about 1¾ lb (0.875 kg).*

Spicy Glazed Pecans

⅓ cup (75 mL) sugar
¼ cup (50 mL) butter
¼ cup (50 mL) water
1 tbsp (15 mL) Worcestershire sauce
1 tbsp (15 mL) seasoned salt
½ tsp (2 mL) freshly ground pepper
¼ tsp (1 mL) garlic powder
¼ tsp (1 mL) ground cumin
⅛ tsp (0.5 mL) cayenne pepper
4 cups (1 L) pecan halves

Preheat oven to 350°F (180°C). Line a large rimmed baking sheet with parchment paper or nonstick foil.

Place all ingredients except pecans in a large saucepan. Bring to a boil over medium heat, stirring frequently. Add pecans and cook, stirring frequently, until pecans are thickly coated with sugar mixture, about 5 minutes. Spread pecan mixture in a single layer in prepared pan.

Bake, stirring twice, for 15 minutes or until pecans are richly glazed. Cool completely in pan on a rack. Store in an airtight container in a cool dry place for up to 1 week or freeze for up to 1 month. *Makes 4 cups (1 L).*

Safety Matters

Most furnaces won't operate during a power outage. Stay warm by gathering family members in a room with a fireplace or other safe source of indoor heating. Dress in layers and close blinds and drapes to keep heat from escaping.

For more safety tips, visit www.atcogas.com.

POINSETTIAS

Poinsettias are a favourite Christmas plant. They will hold their leaves better and stay lush and green if the soil is kept slightly moist and the plant is kept away from drafts.

CLASSIC NUTS AND BOLTS

3 cups (750 mL) corn and rice cereal
3 cups (750 mL) crisp oat cereal circles
3 cups (750 mL) whole wheat cereal squares
3 cups (750 mL) fish-shaped cheese crackers
3 cups (750 mL) pretzel sticks
½ cup (125 mL) unsalted blanched peanuts
1 cup (250 mL) butter
2 tbsp (25 mL) Worcestershire sauce
1 tbsp (15 mL) fresh lemon juice
2 tsp (10 mL) hot pepper sauce
2 tsp (10 mL) onion powder
1 tsp (5 mL) garlic powder
1 tsp (5 mL) celery salt
½ tsp (2 mL) cayenne pepper
½ tsp (2 mL) salt

Preheat oven to 250°F (120°C). Combine first 6 ingredients (corn and rice cereal through peanuts) in a large roasting pan; set aside.

Melt butter in a small saucepan over medium heat. Whisk in next 8 ingredients (Worcestershire sauce through salt) until blended. Pour butter mixture over cereal mixture and toss gently to coat.

Bake, stirring every 30 minutes, for 2 hours. Cool completely in pan on a rack. Store in an airtight container in a cool dry place for up to 1 week or freeze for up to 1 month. *Makes about 14 cups (3.5 L).*

 Cook's Note: *ATCO Blue Flame Kitchen used Kellogg's Crispix Krispies Cereal, General Mills Cheerios Cereal, Post Shreddies Cereal and Pepperidge Farm Cheddar Goldfish Baked Snack Crackers in this recipe.*

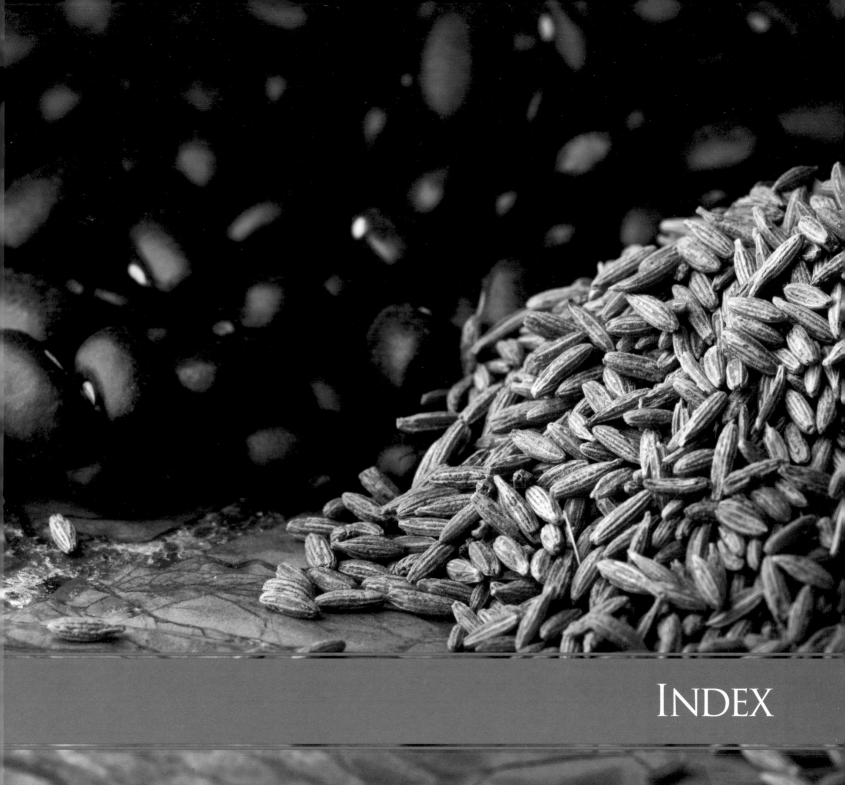

INDEX

ATCO GAS

ATCO Gas, an Alberta-based, province-wide natural gas distribution company, has provided Albertans with safe, reliable natural gas service for more than 100 years. Today, ATCO Gas serves more than one million customers in nearly 300 Alberta communities.

ATCO Gas provides safety information and optional safety checks to assist customers in ensuring the safety of their internal systems and appliances. Call our Customer Assistance Centre at 310.5678 or visit www.atcogas.com for information.

ATCO Gas also provides expert advice and energy safety, conservation and efficiency information through ATCO EnergySense and ATCO Blue Flame Kitchen. For more information, visit www.atcoenergysense.com and www.atcoblueflamekitchen.com.

ATCO Gas is on call 24-hours a day, 365 days a year to respond immediately to all natural gas emergency calls, including no heat, gas odour or carbon monoxide. If you smell natural gas, leave the building or area immediately and call 911 or **ATCO Gas's 24-hour emergency contact number** for your area using a landline (not a cellular phone).

Edmonton and Area: 780.420.5585
Calgary and Area: 403.245.7222
Elsewhere in Alberta: 1.800.511.3447